MW00470751

The Sky Stretched Out Before Me

For Eileen Grimes,

With appreciation for your good work

much love,
Ray

2-12-2021

The Sky
Stretched Out
Before Me

Encounters with Mystics,
Anomalies, and Waking Dreams

Ray Grasse

Inner Eye Publications/Chicago, Illinois 2020

Also by Ray Grasse:

The Waking Dream: Unlocking the Symbolic Language of Our Lives

Signs of the Times: Unlocking the Symbolic Language of World Events

Under a Sacred Sky: Essays on the Philosophy and Practice of Astrology

An Infinity of Gods: Conversations with an Unconventional Mystic

Urban Mystic: Recollections of Goswami Kriyananda

StarGates: Essays on Astrology, Symbolism, and the Synchronistic Universe

Copyright © 2020 Ray Grasse

All rights reserved. No part of this book may be used or reproduced in any manner
(with the exception of quotations embodied in critical articles or reviews) without
written permission from the author and publisher.

All photos (including cover) © Ray Grasse unless otherwise specified.

Typeset by Amnet Systems

Inner Eye Publications | Chicago, Illinois

For Lacey, Marcus, Sean and Makaila – I love you all

TABLE OF CONTENTS

ACKNOWLEDGEMENTS

I want to express my deepest gratitude to all those who offered feedback, support or inspiration during the writing of this book, including Judith Wiker, Laurence Hillman, Barbara Keller, Allison Gawor, Bess Demopolous, Bill Hogan, Sharon Harms, Normandi Ellis, Richard Smoley, Dave Gunning, Elizabeth Avedon, Sharon George, Debby Sher, Kevin Korody, Siri Oftedahl, Greg Taylor, Eric and Devi Klein, Dav Ero, Gale Ahrens, Gary Lachman, Dany Petrova, Kirsty Jackson, Diane and Mike Burdorf, Greg Bogart, Jane Wodening, Al Paoletti, Richard Tarnas, John David Ebert, Paula Finnegan, Doyle Armbrust, Sharon Steffensen, Russell Taylor, Mia Feroleto, Maureen Cleary, Victoria Martin, Bill Hunt, Anthony Wright and, most of all, my parents Raymond and Catherine, to whom I owe everything.

INTRODUCTION

I wasn't yet a teenager when I happened to catch a screening on TV of Alfred Hitchcock's *Spellbound*, with its celebrated dream sequence designed by Salvador Dali. I'd never seen anything like that before—not during waking hours, anyway—with its amalgam of surrealistic imagery that included the specter of giant eyes floating in the sky and a man running down the side of a pyramid beneath the menacing shadow of giant wings. Mind-blowing stuff, that.

It was mystifying, but for that same reason it seared it itself permanently into my brain. Aside from igniting a long-term fascination with both surrealism and Salvador Dali (and later, even experimental film, which drew largely from the same well), it was the first time I actually recall being consciously aware of *symbols*, even if I didn't know that's what they were called. I immediately recognized their extraordinary impact on the imagination. There was no logic at all to them, but that was precisely their appeal. It was as if they spoke a language beyond words—a language that might even hold important secrets into the universe, I suspected. There was an "otherness" about them which hinted at an otherness to the world itself. Plus, those images were *beautiful*, which likely sank their pylons even deeper into my subconscious.

It was a number of years later during freshman year in college when a fellow student named Debby told me about an enigmatic little volume called *The Emerald Tablet of Hermes Trismesgistus*. She said it was handed down from an ancient Egyptian source, and was the subject of much discussion in esoteric and alchemical circles. Only much later did I learn that claims about its origins might not be entirely true; but that didn't really matter, any more than learning that a line of great poetry wasn't really "true," or that the Dali dream sequence wasn't "true." A few of us students at the time thought ourselves fairly cool since we were reading the works of writers like Antonin Artaud, Carlos Castenada, and Krishnamurti, among others. But this was something altogether different. The words in that little volume haunted me, and one line in particular jumped off the page:

As Above, So Below

For some reason, it reminded me of that dream sequence in the Hitchcock/Dali film from years earlier, and set me thinking about symbols in my own life. Were the things, people, and events around me somehow a reflection of deeper or higher realities? If true, the implications seemed boundless.

As a result of influences like these, my attitude towards reality itself was slowly changing. Rather than see the world as something solid or completely external, I was beginning to suspect it was bound up somehow with the mind, with *consciousness*. That notion came to its startling climax with a dramatic lucid dream I had one night where I became aware that I was dreaming, while still in the dream. I recall looking around and seeing every tiny detail in my environment, every blade of grass, which was astonishing to me. I'd seen many Hollywood movies where dreams were depicted in foggy or hazy ways, yet this was anything but foggy of hazy. I even stomped down on the grass with my foot at one point in the dream, just to see how tangible and real everything was, and thought to myself, "My God...*This is every bit as 'real' as waking life!"* I woke up from that dream in a state of amazement, thinking that if my dream could seem that real, who's to say my waking life is any less of a dream?

That experience eventually became one of several inspirations for the essays and books I'd later write where I explored the dreamlike nature not just of personal life but of our collective culture. I was fascinated by the secret language of symbols, and began a systematic study of symbolic, mythological and divinatory systems from around the world. I was intrigued to find certain recurring elements and themes weaving through many of them, and labored to find a synthesizing framework that might tie those varied elements together.

This book explores a number of those ideas and themes. It isn't so much an autobiography as it is a series of *autobiographical sketches*, using certain key episodes from my life to discuss broader issues and ideas that have been important to me through the years. The stories recounted here circle back time and again to several basic questions, such as: *Are there deeper patterns or archetypal forces shaping our lives? What are we to make of extraordinary coincidences, or what Carl Jung called synchronicities? What does it mean when we encounter "weird" events in our lives? Is there more to reality than we think? And last but not least, who—or what—am I?*

I don't pretend to offer definitive answers to any of these questions, but I do hope the following chapters will have you thinking about them in some new and hopefully creative ways.

—Ray Grasse, 2020

CHAPTER 1

THE WIND AND THE WAVES

1977

Streaks of cirrus clouds drifted overhead while the sound of bird-songs echoed in the distance. I was seated in the front of a canoe, part of a group of six young men paddling through the Minnesota Boundary Waters near the Canadian border. We were miles away from civilization and hadn't seen anyone else for days by this point. I'd been invited to come along on this trip a few weeks earlier when another member dropped out, so here I was, taking in the sights and sounds of this remote patch of wilderness. The entire scene looked like something out of the pre-industrial past, and in a curious way I almost felt like I was *in* the past.

Just as I was turning around to say something to my canoe partner, Bill, I caught sight of another canoe slowly pulling up alongside ours. These were the first people we'd seen in days, and inside that canoe were two young men dressed in full retro-regalia, buckskin hats and suede clothing laced with fringe, looking like veteran trappers who had just stepped out of the 18th Century. It was refreshing to see other people at this point, however anachronistic, and as they glided slowly past our boat I exchanged a few words with the lead paddler in theirs. We talked briefly about our experiences up to that point, which is when I started to notice that he was squinting intently at me, as if trying to place my face.

Finally, he asked, "Say...Aren't you Ray Grasse?"

I was startled, and replied, yes, that's me. But how could he possibly know who I am?

"I met you at Bill Kavanagh's house party last fall. I'm Mark. We had a conversation about music."

Ah, yes, now I remembered. We had a fun talk, but it didn't last more than fifteen minutes, so I was surprised he remembered me at all. Just like I was surprised that we could bump into one another out there, six hundred miles away from both our homes. We continued exchanging pleasantries for a few more minutes until he and his partner finally pulled ahead in their canoe and disappeared off into the marshland and tall weeds, never to be seen again.

That exchange took place during a time when I was becoming increasingly interested in coincidences and the strange intersections of fate that weave throughout our lives. Experiences like these were a part of the reason I came to believe there really was a hidden design beneath the surface of everyday life. In a sense, I started to feel as though *everything interlocked*.

Several days later, as our trip drew to a close and we rowed back to the launch site, I ambled up onto a nearby rocky bluff with another team member, Mike, and the two of us took a moment to look out over the waterway we'd just paddled in from. The wind was blowing across the surface of the water and creating the kinds of wave patterns one sees on bodies of water when the wind blows strong. It was while staring at one small spot on the water's surface that I first noticed it: the seeming chaos and choppiness of the waves concealed a deeper order. As I pulled back and broadened my perspective just a bit, I realized there were actually three or four wave fronts converging onto that small spot, and that it was actually the intersection of those wave fronts that gave rise to the *illusion* of choppiness and chaos, of ripplets sprouting to and fro in seemingly random fashion. But if I looked more carefully, I could see there was nothing random or chaotic about it at all, and I saw that now with sterling clarity.

Simple as it was, this struck me with the force of revelation, largely because it resonated so powerfully with what I had been thinking about lately. Viewed up close, the situations in my life often appeared chaotic and random, but if I stood back far enough, I could tell those developments really consisted of broader "wave fronts" that were converging onto singular moments in time and space—whether I chose to call those "wave fronts" archetypes, planets, gods, numbers, or something else entirely. Whatever label I assigned them, I had no doubt those patterns were actually very orderly, and that a profound structure lie behind all the chaos. There were just too many strange happenings and recurring themes in my life for me to think otherwise—like the coincidence of that fellow in the passing canoe just a few days earlier. If I could "peer behind the curtain" just a bit further, I thought, I felt sure that I would see coincidences like that one happening all the time. I turned to Mike and cautiously shared my thoughts with him about all this with him, unsure of what he'd think. I was happy to see he not only understood what I was saying, but seemed genuinely interested.

Just one hour later, the six of us crawled back into the car we drove there in to begin the long trip back to Illinois. We were exhausted but exhilarated, because it had been great spending that time out in the wild away from civilization, with all its clocks and crowds. But it was tiring, too, since I hadn't had a good night's sleep in days.

As we pulled out onto the highway taking us back to Chicago, my friend Dave reached over and turned on the radio, as I let the jangled rhythms of civilization start washing over me.

CHAPTER 2

MEETINGS WITH REMARKABLE MEN

I t all began with music.

My mother once explained how she played the piano every day while pregnant with me, and in so doing bathed my amniotic universe with the muffled harmonies of her own unseen worlds. I don't actually recall that, of course, but I have no doubt it played an important role in shaping my lifelong interest in music, and quite possibly my attitude towards life itself.

My earliest years were spent in a suburb of Chicago called Oak Park, a community best known for past residents like Frank Lloyd Wright, Edgar Rice Burroughs and Ernest Hemingway. My mother's childhood friend Catherine Johnston lived in one of Hemingway's early homes, and I spent almost as much time growing up in that house as my own. More than once I'd be sitting in that kitchen eating a meal and wondering about the curious fact I was sitting in the same spot young Ernest undoubtedly sat many times. Our house was a few streets over along the 700 block of Belleforte, a short span of street that somehow retained its original cobblestone paving from a half-century earlier. In some vaguely-defined way, I fancied that this anachronistic stretch of stone paving afforded me talismanic access to that entire neighborhood's colorful past.

My parents were both working class. My father was a carpenter who worked on construction sites in Chicago until he was 70, and my mother was a telephone operator for over 30 years, though her secret passion was doing art and composing music. My dad worked the daytime shift, while mom traded off with him by working evenings at the telephone company. She'd often come home late and continue working on her music and art, drinking cups of coffee to stay awake.

My mother and father, brother Greg (lower left), and me.

They were both liberal in politics but conservative in lifestyle. They smoked cigarettes but rarely drank, and never swore, at least not in front of me. The one time I lost control of my own mouth and screamed *"Asshole!"* at my brother during a heated argument in the living room, my parents looked like they were ready to call an exorcist. But apart from outbursts like that, I was a painfully shy kid; even stepping outside of the house was always a major challenge, and social interactions were a source of deep dread.

Neither my mom or dad were especially religious, but my Pisces mother had a strong spiritual side and my Gemini father was a 32nd degree Mason, so they both had their guiding principles. They decided to send my brother and I to a Lutheran school in nearby River Forest, hoping this would afford us better moral guidance than we'd receive in a public school. That was, and remains, a dubious hope.

While there were some good elements to that parochial exposure—especially the school's emphasis on the arts and music—I was far too influenced by the darker implications of those beliefs, with their surreal notions of heaven and hell and the ghastly doctrine of original sin. Concepts like these saddled me early on with a sense of guilt regarding anything involving personal pleasure or happiness, while also sadding me with a distorted sense of God which discouraged me from entertaining any thoughts about the possibility divinity might lie somewhere within. It was a herculean task breaking loose from the moorings of those early influences those next few years, but I finally did so, with the help of two things in particular.

The first was psychedelics. Initially, I was frightened by the potential dangers of LSD, due to alarmist articles I'd read in the press that included stories of people jumping out of windows, losing their minds, and other such horrors. But at age 18 I finally decided to give it a try. These were the days when LSD was not only fairly easy to come by but still relatively pure and untainted by additives. I have no idea where things stand now, but the last time I tried LSD, 35 years ago, it felt like it was spiked with amphetamines, which made for a very unpleasant, jaw-clenching "trip."

At its best, LSD was fascinating for the way it seemed to peel away layers of fossilized preconceptions and allowed me to see ordinary things with fresh eyes again, almost like a child. A simple cloud might radiate luminosity, while the sounds of the wind blowing through the trees seemed utterly unique, as though I could perceive the individual micro-frequencies of the sounds themselves. Most important of all, it showed me that my ordinary mind wasn't the only window through which to perceive the world, and that there was far more to reality—and myself—than I could have imagined.

The other seismic influence on my life during those years involved several remarkable spiritual teachers I crossed paths with. The lure of exotic knowledge from the East had been wafting through the culture for some time by that point; in addition to the flood of volumes on mystical and metaphysical topics that began appearing on bookstore shelves, it wasn't unusual to turn on a talk show then and see a celebrated yogi speaking with late-night host Johnny Carson about the benefits of meditation, or hear some movie star talk about their Sun-signs. So there was nothing particularly odd about a Midwestern teenager like myself start turning away from his conventional religious upbringing and begin looking to faraway sources for the answers to life's pressing questions.

And so at 19, during sophomore year at college, I first began studying under a spiritual teacher, Goswami Kriyananda (birth name: Melvin Higgins). He was a Chicago-born yogi in the Kriya Yoga tradition, and ran a modest-sized center in the heart of the city which offered classes, lectures, and personal instruction to students on a variety of esoteric topics.

Though I never became a disciple—not of his or anyone else, for that matter—I wound up studying with him for 15 years in all, and had the chance to spend time with him outside of classes and lectures on a number of occasions. As I described in *Urban Mystic*, I came to regard him as a deeply insightful mystic with a special gift for distilling profound teachings into simple terms, such as: "Everyone's striving for God, when they haven't even found their humanness yet"; or, "Your earth life *is* your spiritual life"; or "There can be no such thing as 'failure' if you do what you do because you enjoy it." But then there were more cryptic comments like this:

> "You can look down from the vantage point of the Third Eye and see everybody else's material and mental realms. From that vantage point you see an infinite number of sidereal universes, and surrounding each spark of God is built a universe."

In some ways, though, it was the teachings and philosophy of *his* teacher, Shelly Trimmer, that wound up having an even greater impact on me. I say that largely because Shelly's teachings were the basis for much of what Kriyananda taught; as Kriyananda himself often said, "All my teachings ultimately stem from Shelly." Shelly was the fountainhead.

Born in 1917 and died in 1996, Shelly studied with the famed yogi Paramahansa Yogananda during the early 1940s, and went on to live a comparatively private life, marrying and raising a family, working part-time in an electronics store, and teaching largely on a one-to-one basis with a very small number of students. As an editor and writer, I've been lucky during the course of my life to know quite a few brilliant thinkers, but Shelly was undoubtedly the most interesting—and impressive—of them all. His knowledge of meditation, magic, the chakras, astrology, science, and other topics, dazzled me.

But I was struck by how little of that knowledge seemed to have come from books. With some exceptions, his insights on spiritual and occult matters seemed to be based on personal insight and experience rather than drawn from philosophy texts. His grasp of symbolism, and the symbolic dimensions of life in general, proved especially integral to my own thinking over the years, yet he was always careful to ground those ideas in the practical realities of everyday experience.

Fascinating, too—if a bit unsettling—was how he would make little passing comments now and then which suggested he knew far more about me than he rightly should have. Out of the blue, he'd hint at an experience from my past or some private concern which I'd never spoken about to anyone. How was *that* possible, I wondered? On returning from my first trip to see Shelly, I asked Kriyananda about this, to which he smiled and said, "Oh, he knows a *lot* about people even before he meets them in person."

The first time I met him was in September of 1977, while I was still in my mid-20s—just several weeks after my experience in the Boundary Waters, in fact. Looking back on it with the benefit of hindsight, I've realized how much of a turning point that first meeting was for me. I've written about my conversations with him in *An Infinity of Gods,* and won't try to recap all of that here. What I thought I'd do instead is simply present a small cross-section of those conversations with him, which will convey something of my relationship with him over the years and the scope of our wide-ranging conversations.

⋙╬⋘

RAY: Why did God create us in the first place?

SHELLY TRIMMER: First of all, God *did not* create you, spiritually. Because if you had a beginning, you of necessity had an end. So you always were. Now, you are in the *image* of God, and *like unto* God. But this does not mean he created you. You are self-conscious awareness, like God is self-conscious awareness. God is a being like you are. He's a being of self-conscious awareness. You are a self-existent one. You always were, you always will be, you cannot be destroyed.

RAY: Are there many beings like God?

SHELLY: Oh, yes, yes.

RAY: So he was one of many beings of that nature, but was the first one to become illuminated?

SHELLY: He's the first one to become illuminated *in this way.* And he has many disciples, and they go around keeping balance in his cosmic dream. Remember, all that come in by his grace to learn his technique are imbalanced, and they can tear the fabric of his dream and of his memory track to pieces—unless they're kept in sort of order. So we're very *restricted.* Look at how you are restricted, in all sorts of ways, so that your state of imbalance doesn't go too far.

God is a being like you are. He's a being of self-conscious awareness. What is the difference between you and God, or any being who has self-conscious awareness at any particular point in space or time? There is just one difference: the *degree of balance*. God is a high degree of balanced self-conscious awareness; you are not. You are a very high degree of *un*balance. But we all are.

RAY: If we are really *all* gods, with godlike potential, then why aren't we taught anything like that in our Western religions?

SHELLY: Who would want to teach a religion that doesn't require priests, pastors, rabbis, or institutions? You can't control people with a religion like that.

I was my late 20s when the following exchange took place, and I had just started to try my hand at writing. I was swept up in the ideas I was exploring then, feeling impatient to get my work out into the world, rough and undeveloped as it was at that point. Shelly saw the impatience—and egotism—of that, and questioned me about it.

SHELLY: Why do you feel rushed?

RAY: I don't want to see this work just fall by the wayside.

SHELLY: Why do you worry about that?

RAY: (pause) Because I'd like it to be read, I think it has something to offer.

SHELLY: You see, I don't care what anybody thinks about what I say.

RAY: Well…that's my own neurosis, I guess.

SHELLY: I know. (laughs) You see, I figure I have an eternity to do what I want to do—a whole eternity. So I feel no rush whatsoever. That I'm not going to live long enough to do it in this life doesn't bother me in the slightest. I don't care at all (laughs loudly)! In fact, truly, I've said most of the things I wanted to say in this life. It's there on tapes, if somebody wants to listen to them. Besides, if I don't do it or say it, somebody else will.

RAY: Is that really true, though? If I didn't write a certain book or paint a certain painting, would somebody else have done it?

SHELLY: If it was important, yes.

RAY: If it was important?

SHELLY: Yes. When the time comes for an invention, haven't you noticed how it's invented all over the world simultaneously?

RAY: But those inventions are different from one another.

SHELLY: Oh, no they're not.

RAY: I've never seen two paintings that looked the same.

SHELLY: Maybe not exactly the same, no. But they're still portraying the same ideas. Otherwise why would a nation limit somebody so that they couldn't paint a certain idea or theme? Like in Russia, artists are restricted, they're allowed to paint certain ideas and not others. (This conversation took place in 1978, before the collapse of the Soviet Union.) Writers as well. So there are all different kinds of systems of painting, all different forms of artwork. And there's always someone to express it.

Of course, each one of us likes to think that we're very important, and without us it wouldn't have taken place. This is especially true of politicians. They figure that the world can't get along without them. But history has proven again and again the world gets along quite well without them. In fact, it probably would have gotten along better if they hadn't existed. But the politician doesn't think so! He thinks about how *important* he is.

SHELLY: Yogananda told me that when one of his disciples was dying, she made him promise he could come and see that she was all right over there. Now, he had a little difficulty finding her, since it's not very easy finding someone over there, and when he found her, he called out to her—several times, in fact. In her semi-dreamlike state she was tending a garden, but she looked up at him, and thanked him for coming. Of course when he came, she woke up just a *little* bit more, but then she went back to her semi-sleep stage and continued gardening. You see, we gravitate to those things over there which suit us, in other words. Another example would be a man who worked hard all his life. He might just sit and rock back and forth in his rocker, because his idea of heaven would be not having to go to work. See?

So they're in a semi-dreamlike state, and like a broken record they run over the important events in their life. Eventually the sum total of their life experience causes them to desire to be reincarnated again. And they are drawn—instinctively, you might say—to the new body which is contiguous with their nature, so that their astrological code and their genetic code is a representation of their natures and expresses their particular level of balanced self-conscious awareness. So that they don't feel like a fish out of water, see? As it is, we are all a little bit alone in this world anyhow, we feel just a little bit like we're a fish out of water. This is basically a lonely place. You're born alone and you die alone; it doesn't matter how many people are around you.

⇒┤├⇐

RAY: I recall you saying that when most people go into the astral world, they see their own preconceived ideas, and not what's actually there. So how does one see what's actually there?

SHELLY: By being a disinterested observer.

RAY: And then you will naturally gravitate towards what's really there?

SHELLY: Yes. And if you see something that emotionally disturbs you, you're caught. From then on you start dreaming, and you no longer see reality as it is. So you want to be an observer and not controlled by what you're seeing. Many people go into the astral, and see exactly what they thought it would be. That is true of virtually all who go there. It's very hard to find truth in the astral world. It's easier to find it here than it is there, because over there you usually find your own preconceived ideas. In the astral world everything will be what you want it to be, because you're creating it. Even *here,* you're going about dreaming a lot of dreams and not seeing reality as it truly is, you're making it the way you want to be. But it's a little bit harder to mold reality here than it is in the astral world.

This is why, when you go into the astral world, you remain an observer—that is, you become only 10 percent interested or less.

Actually, it should be one twelfth, but 10 percent is adequate; you have to remain less than 10 percent interested. Because if you become any more interested in that, then you become involved, you're beginning to take part—and now you're lost as an impartial observer. You are now influencing the phenomenon, and the phenomena is influencing you. You have stepped over that boundary. Likewise, when a person comes to you for information or advice, and you get over 10 percent interested in their life, you begin to live their life for them. And you know what happens when somebody tries to live your life for you!

⚛

RAY: Is the leader of a country the personification of that country, and the general mood of that country?

SHELLY: That is what many astrologers say. If he or she doesn't represent the sum total of the mood of the people at that time, then he couldn't remain in office. And so he or she symbolically represents the total karma of the people at that time.

And the ruler of a country is a very enslaved individual. Because he is not free to do what he wants to do, he is controlled more or less by the oversoul of that country.

RAY: Is he any less free than anyone else?

SHELLY: Yes, he's much less free. If you want to seek freedom, don't ever take a position of authority.

RAY: How about someone like a rock-and-roll idol, like one of the Beatles? That's not "authority" in the sense that a president or head of a company is, but they're having a massive influence on people.

SHELLY: That's still authority, an authority of that type of influence that he has over people.

RAY: They're being molded almost more by the cultural needs of that time?

SHELLY: Yes. This is what makes them so successful. They're adaptable to the cultural needs of the people at that time. And what they're feeling is what the people needed; if what they were feeling and expressing wasn't what the people wanted, they wouldn't have succeeded.

RAY: So each famous person is in danger of losing some of their free will because of being in the limelight?

SHELLY: That's right.

RAY: What about Yogananda?

SHELLY: He felt very enslaved. There was a time I'd been watching him as people were coming in, you know, and they were talking to him. He said to me, "This might look wonderful to you—how important I am, people coming in and asking me all kind of questions, to solve all their problems for them, telling them what to do, and what not to do, and how they wait in line to see me. But I am not free. I am enslaved."

He told me on another occasion about going down to Mexico three times (to take a break from the responsibilities of his organization). He said, "I know now that the only way I'm going to be free is when I die, when I leave this body. That's the only way I can be free. My karma won't let me be free any other way."

16

Then he added, "I must free as many people as I enslaved as a result of my last incarnation"—he believed he was William the Conqueror in his last incarnation. And he said, "I enslaved many people as a result of that, and I've got to free as many people as I enslaved." Not the same ones, but as many people. Then he said, "You! You remain free! Don't you get involved like I have."

And I listened to him.

━━╬ ╬━━

RAY: You seemed to have had a beautiful marriage.

SHELLY: They say true love doesn't run smooth, but that's a lot of baloney. My wife and I hardly ever had any disturbances in our life together. It's almost like what you read about in the fairy tales: "... and they lived happily ever after." The only real thing we had any disagreement about was our schedules; I was more of a night person and preferred to get up later in the morning, and she was more or a morning person and got up earlier. But that really wasn't a big issue. Like my one daughter said once, of all the people that she knows, her mother and me were the only people who ever seemed really happy.

RAY: Is there a secret to keeping a relationship happy like that?

SHELLY: For men, the most important thing is probably this: men think that if they go out and buy a $15,000 car for a woman, that will mean a lot to her. But for many women, they'll be even more moved by a three-dollar card you send her with a love note in it than by that $15,000 car.

RAY: Pay attention to the little things. In other words, it's the little gestures?

SHELLY: Yes. Maybe even go out and buy a little black book, and mark down the day you met her. Put down the first day you had a date with her, you made out with her, you held her hand—all these little things, these are important. Above all else, write down her birthday. And remember Christmas, the day you got married, your song—put all these down.

RAY: On the other side of the fence, what would you say to a woman about dealing with the man in her life?

SHELLY: The main thing for her is realize that her husband is a big baby. Now, he thinks he's real strong, of course. You see, when a man gets sick, he's seriously ill. But from a man's point of view, when a woman gets sick it's just a minor thing. But there doesn't have to be very much wrong with a man for him to think it's really bad. And his ego is quite fragile, so he doesn't like it to be torn apart or criticized too much. So he's a great big baby, though he doesn't want to admit it. He needs a lot of attention in his own way, and a building up of his ego.

But also it's important that the woman let the husband know that he doesn't have to go somewhere else to get sex. This is very important for a man: that she's willing to make love to him, and that she doesn't have a headache every night that he needs sex. But men also have to realize that a woman does not get sexually aroused as quickly as a man does. This is important. A woman is nowhere near as driven by sex as a man is. And there is many a married woman who's never actually been aroused by her husband. A woman is very slow to be aroused. A man should take at least fifteen or twenty minutes to get his wife excited before he makes love to her, because this is generally how long it takes before she can reach some degree of desire. If he comes on like a lot of men do like, "I wanna make love, honey!"— wham, bam, thank you, ma'am— and that's the end of it, you know. I've known a lot of women who never knew any sexual enjoyment with their first husbands, and didn't experience any satisfaction at all until they became involved with an older man. And of course with a second marriage, the man is generally older than the first one so he's not as "quick on the trigger" as a younger man would be. So she may even find she loves her second husband better than the first one, because he gives her an emotional satisfaction she never got from her first husband.

And a man should learn some control, so that the lovemaking isn't over just about when it starts to get interesting for the woman. So that if he learns self-control—and the technique of Kriya will give him a great deal of self-control in this particular matter—he can reach a climax the same time as she does. If he can manage this, then she will feel far more satisfied and have a stronger loving desire towards him. But if he has a climax at some other time, it doesn't bring them anywhere near as close in their relationship. So he should use control, and watch her stimulation so that he reaches a climax when she does.

SHELLY: The Self must forever meditate upon itself (i.e., contemplate its own nature) in order to sustain the Self. It's through this act of Self-reflection that the Self not only regenerates its own existence, but all of the existences of which it is aware. It has always done so, and will forever do so, for were the Self to ever cease meditating upon itself, it would cease to be. And if this could happen unto one's own spiritual being, it could happen to all. And in the infinities of existence, if it could happen to one, it would have already happened unto all—and you would not now be here listening to this.

RAY: You once said that each of us exists simultaneously within time as well as beyond time; we're both finite and transfinite at the same time. How is that possible?

SHELLY: OK, let's take a photon. A photon leaves the Sun, and from our perspective it takes eight minutes to reach the earth. But from the standpoint of the photon itself, it arrives at Earth the same moment it leaves the Sun, because there is no time whatsoever at the speed of light. And if there is no time, there is no space. So it's all relative to the state of awareness. Time and space are not like you are aware of them here.

This next exchange was intriguing to me in the way Shelly made a clear distinction between ecstasy and bliss, and how the former could be attained via extreme or artificial means, whereas bliss was the end result of genuine spiritual, meditative practice. I gathered from his comments that bliss involves an element of stillness not generally found in experiences of ecstasy.

SHELLY: When the viewer becomes the viewed, when the lover becomes the loved, when the beholder becomes the beheld, the feeling is one of pure unadulterated bliss—"ever-new, ever- changing, ever more glorious bliss." If you think drugs are a way, this is far above and beyond that. All drugs can really do is lead you into the illusions of the astral world, and perhaps into some form of ecstasy. But not bliss, which is different from ecstasy, and is nothing like the "peace that goeth before all understanding." It's not the pool which is clear, in which you can see reality as it really is. Remember: all of us, we pretend we are one thing, but we're really something else. But in the clear pool, we see reality and ourselves as it all really is. In so doing we move towards the great purpose of existence, the very nature of our being.

≒╂╅

RAY: There are mystics who suggest that there are races of beings in the universe far more evolved that humans. Even some scientists have theorized about that, too, something called the Kardashev scale. So my question is, if such beings actually exist and really are that much more evolved than we, why are they still even on the physical plane? If they were *that* evolved, wouldn't they have transcended the physical universe entirely?

SHELLY: That's quite easy. The path towards God consciousness is *not the path of the wheel.* [The "wheel" refers to the wheel of rebirth, the astral and physical realms associated with the subtle energy channels on the right and left-hand sides of the spine, otherwise known as Ida and Pingala.] And those beings are still on the path of the wheel. On the path of the wheel, there are beings of *tremendous* power, *tremendous* elevation. Compared to us, they're almost like gods. But they're still on *the path of the wheel,* and they are not on the *path of the saint.* Which is an entirely different thing.

RAY: What is the path of the saint?

SHELLY: You see, a saint is not a "powerful" being. A saint is more Christlike in his or her characteristics. A saint moves by the *path* *of the seven,* not by the *path of the twelve.* If you move by the path of the twelve, that takes millions of years to reach God consciousness. You can eventually evolve to where you are the controller of a whole solar system, or the controller of a galaxy, and then of an entire universe or a cosmos. In other words, you keep climbing up the ladder through the echelons of control. But that is *the path of the twelve.*

RAY: So the path of the seven is cutting through the center of the wheel?

SHELLY: Yes. That is the path of Sushumna [the channel of consciousness located within the center of the spine]. This is why they said God loved seven above all other numbers, because it's the path of balance, the straight and the narrow. It's a path that's easy to fall off of, because you can get so interested in something happening either in Ida or Pingala that you lose your balance.

⪥⊹⪤

RAY: Suppose someone doesn't have access to spiritual teachers in the physical world. Is there somewhere on the astral where they can go to get this knowledge, where they can find great teachers?

SHELLY: If you divide up what are called "astral planes"—or the world of Yetzirah (using Kabbalistic terms)—and divide it into seven planes, then the fifth plane would be where they have all the colleges, the schools of leaning.

RAY: Is that where the devas [angelic beings] hang out?

SHELLY: Well, some of them are above that. On the fifth plane, human beings still look like human beings. And there are an enormous number of colleges and teachers there. And the method of teaching is...well, a lot of it is under a tree. It's very beautiful there and in the open, like maybe how the Greek philosophers taught. They even have research labs where they do great amount of experimenting and research work. You can learn almost anything you want there. And many people go to those colleges when they sleep every night, or between lifetimes.

In the lower planes, you're *so* controlled by desires that you haven't got any real freedom at all. Your animalistic nature is in complete domination of your awareness.

RAY: Are we talking here about the first and second planes?

SHELLY: Yes. And the third plane. Those three run you almost completely. And on the fifth plane, the individual—if they're in the higher part of the fifth plane, anyway—might not reincarnate at all, unless they want to. Or there might be a long period between reincarnations before a desire comes back to balance out factors within his or her nature. But if you go up above that to the sixth or the seventh planes, they no longer even look like humanoids.

RAY: They're like balls of light?

SHELLY: Yeah, they're balls of light. And if you speak about the Earth to them, they're not even *interested* in what's going on down here. (laughs) So these beings won't reincarnate any more, unless they choose to come back perhaps as a great teacher, or as an avatar.

RAY: Do they do that?

SHELLY: Oh yeah, they'll do that. You see, this is an act of unselfish love which helps them advance further. Because they're still in the astral realms and they want to go into the world of Christ consciousness. But they haven't advanced *that* far yet.

⊶‡⊷

SHELLY: The natural habitat of all life is in deep space, not on the gravity worlds. On the gravity worlds, our memory banks are heavily restricted, so that we naturally forget who we really are, *you do not know that you are any place but here.* But if you become aware that you are, so that you can say, "I am blissfully aware that I am," you are then wherever you *want* to be—which can be outside the cosmic dream of God, or in here, or wherever you desire to be. You are no longer restricted by the animal body.

⊶‡⊷

RAY: Are you just a thought in my mind, or do you have an independent existence of your own?

SHELLY: (Pause) Both.

⊶‡⊷

RAY: If you knew that you were going to die shortly and you were asked to sum up your life teachings in one final statement, what would you say?

SHELLY: Very simple. To those who came to my funeral, I'd say this: take three minutes of meditation to prove that this is the way. Because it is the path, truly, to God consciousness. Even if there is no God, the technique of meditation leads to a very favorable degree of self-conscious awareness. And this is well worth it, because this is controlled awareness; you are always placing everything in its correct order, all the experiences that come into you. And the experiences that come to you are therefore blissful, rather than there sometimes being experiences which are painful because you haven't placed them into balanced order. That's what meditation leads to.

Anyone who has gone any depth at all into meditation becomes aware that it is the golden path, the way in which the alchemists are changing base lead into spiritual gold. You're climbing up the ladder, what the Bible calls Jacob's ladder, and it is the expression of the law of self-conscious awareness. And that's true for all beings in existence who have self-conscious awareness. What is the difference between God and you at any given moment or place in time? Only one: he is complete balanced self-conscious awareness. And these basics are true throughout all existence. All the other stuff that I say, those can be variables, because they're just musings about things. But it's the basics that are important.

One last thing. During the years I studied with Kriyananda, I apparently came to be regarded by some of his disciples as somewhat eccentric, if not a bit weird, judging from some of the comments that filtered back to me from time to time. I generally got along with the others, but I could tell some of them didn't quite know what to make of me (and the fact that I felt so socially awkward much of the time surely didn't help matters). It was in the midst of that period my friend Dave Blair told me about the time he went down to Florida to talk with Shelly when my name came up in the course of conversation. Dave light-heartedly asked Shelly, "So…what sector of time and space is Ray Grasse from?" As Dave related the story to me, Shelly laughed out loud and simply said, "Ha! Grasse is an *outlaw!*"

To this day I have no idea at what he meant by that. But whatever it was, I can't help but laugh whenever I think back about it.

CHAPTER 3

FILM SCHOOL

The first time I saw Stan Brakhage up on stage before our class in Fullerton Hall, I was interested to hear what he had to say but I knew next to nothing about him or his work. There was definitely something larger-than-life about his presence, accented by that thick swath of salt-and-pepper hair and a Fu Manchu mustache that gave him a vaguely Mongolian appearance. He chose his words carefully, and seemed intelligent. He had deep-set eyes, which was accented by the overhead lighting in the hall.

My other film professor at the school, John Luther-Scofill, said to me before that first class, "I strongly recommend you attend all of his talks." When I asked why, John looked at me with that trademark poker face of his and replied, "He's only the most important experimental filmmaker in the world, that's all"—as if to suggest I was an idiot for not knowing. Which I suppose I was.

That exchange took place during my first year at the School of the Art Institute of Chicago in 1970, not long before I started studying with Kriyananda, and seven years before meeting Shelly. I'd been to the museum any number of times while growing up and was awed by the artworks that graced its walls. I'd been painting for several years by that point myself and fell in love with the entire experience—the smell of the linseed oil, the texture of the paint as it squeezed out of the tube, and most dramatically, the magic of seeing a world of color and form emerge out of a completely blank canvas. From the start I felt surprisingly comfortable working in this medium, as though I'd been doing it for years. I somehow knew how to blend colors, work with perspective, and calculate the way shadows fell across curved surfaces, and other such things. I received a scholarship to the school based on some paintings I'd done in high school, and looked forward to starting there.

The school was a unique learning experience, but not always in the ways I expected. One of the highlights for me was the chance to hear or meet some of the thinkers or artists who dropped by the school to discuss their work, like parapsychologist J.B. Rhine, artist Claes Oldenburg, or composer Philip Glass. While walking into the school one afternoon I passed an elderly woman heading towards the exit, only to have a fellow classmate come up to me a few seconds later and say, "Did you see her? That was Georgia O'Keeffe!" By then she had already disappeared into the throngs of pedestrians outside the building so I was unable to catch up to her and pester her with my questions, but it was still a thrill having seen her at all. Probably the most impactful of those visiting figures involved the time Ram Dass came to school in the autumn of 1971 to promote his just-released book *Be Here Now*. Largely unknown at the time, he sat cross-legged up on the stage, talking extemporaneously about most anything and everything. He was fascinating. It wasn't my first exposure to Eastern thought, but he exploded on the scene with such force of personality and ideas that it pretty much knocked all of us off our feet.

But alas, the art classes themselves at the school were a disappointment. I came there hoping to learn more about classical techniques like glazing and underpainting, but abstract and conceptual art were all the rage, and none of my instructors knew anything about more traditional methods like those, or if they did, they weren't saying. (It's possible that's all changed at the school since then, but I don't know.) The tipping point for me came one morning during freshman year when I brought a canvas to school I'd been working on since leaving high school, a surrealistic painting I titled "Reunion of Elements," influenced by Dali, Leonardo da Vinci, and others. I worked on it through the summer, and finished it early during freshman year.

"Reunion of Elements" - 1970 (oil on canvas)

I was privately happy with it, but felt worried how my teachers would respond to it. It was certainly different from everything else my classmates were doing. When it came time for me to present it to the class, my instructor, a well-known local artist named Ray Yoshida, skewered it in no uncertain terms. *"This is 1970, Ray,"* he said, *"not the Renaissance..."*—and his comments went downhill from there. His open disdain for my work had a withering impact on my 18-year old ego, especially in front of my classmates. That's when I began shifting my allegiance over to filmmaking, since I realized that continuing on with the art classes weren't likely to bear much fruit for me.

But that turn of events had a silver lining. In contrast with the disappointment I felt with the painting department, the film classes I enrolled in made for an extraordinary experience. I'd been tinkering with a movie camera from a young age, making amateur 8mm movies throughout grade school and high school. During the early 1970s, the School of the Art Institute of Chicago had arguably the best independent film program in the world, so for a film-lover like myself it was like entering seventh heaven. The focus was largely, but not strictly, experimental film. Whenever anyone asked me to define what experimental film was, I'd simply explain that it is to conventional cinema what poetry is to prose, with more of a focus on imagination, suggestiveness, and visual artistry than conventional narrative or storytelling.

My first instructor was John Scofill (who later changed his name to John Luther-Scofill), and was followed shortly after by my classes with Brakhage. John's film work had a massive impact on me, and his visual sensibilities were closer to mine in some ways than Stan's. But Stan's influence was broader and his style challenged my sensibilities more dramatically. Over those next few years he treated us to a broad grasp of not just cinema but literature, music, history, and art. He spoke about writers, poets and artists I'd never heard of before, not to mention countless obscure filmmakers whose names have been largely lost to time, many of whom he knew personally. His interests seemed wide-ranging and his productivity jaw-dropping. It puzzled me then—just as it does now—how he managed to create several hundred films while attending to a large family, writing books, and conducting the mountains of research necessary for those lectures, which ranged from discussions of Chaplin, Sergei Eisenstein, Carl Dryer, Fritz Lang, Orson Welles, F.W. Murnau and Jean Cocteau, to works of countless experimental filmmakers from the 1920s up to the present.

At first, Brakhage's own films struck me as strange, sometimes even off-putting, since they employed a visual vocabulary so different from what I had been familiar with in mainstream movies. That included shaky camera movements, abrupt cuts in quick succession, and unexpected emulsion flares and scratches that would have been scrubbed from any mainstream film. I'd sometimes done those sorts of things in my own home movies, but he managed to take all of that and convert it into art somehow. Most interesting of all, there were subtleties in his work that revealed themselves only after multiple viewings.

What I came to realize was that Brakhage was attempting nothing less than a revolution in how we think about film and its possibilities. Rather than rely on narrative storytelling or framing scenes in one-pointed Renaissance perspective, Brakhage was aiming to break free from those earlier conventions and explore the possibilities of film as a medium unto itself. I once heard Stan referred to as the "Picasso of filmmaking," and that's not a bad comparison, I thought, since both artists broke free of earlier visual rules and opened the door for those who followed. I never heard him express an affinity with any spiritual path, but there was something distinctly Zen-like in his approach to vision, the way he looked at things with what some call *beginner's mind*. I suspect that's a big part of the reason he remained so unknown to the larger world, even to many in the movie industry itself. His films didn't pander to conventional notions of beauty or storytelling, nor play on viewer's emotions with cheap sentimentality. Yet I could tell that my consciousness was somehow being altered and lifted up by that play of light being created up on the screen. His wasn't a "beauty" achieved through manipulation and emotional button-pushing but through qualities of light and the alchemy of editing.

The Pleasure Principle

Ahh, there's that word—*manipulation*. Prior to my classes with him, my own approach toward art revolved almost completely around ideals of beauty, with the aim of enveloping viewers' brains in a rapturous haze of sublime pleasure, almost like a mind-altering narcotic.

Brakhage's approach was altogether different. For him, manipulating audiences wasn't just unappealing, it was *immoral*. Alfred Hitchcock once described his approach to directing films as being "an exact science of audience reactions." Brakhage's attitude couldn't have been further away from that. He felt that great art should never manipulate viewers towards predetermined ends, whether in service of fear, excitement, or even beauty. True art is inherently ambiguous and so vast in scope that it leaves itself open to many reactions. Years later I'd hear Joseph Campbell explain how writer James Joyce considered any artwork that manipulated viewers to be "pornographic." Interesting way to describe it, I thought.

This is also one of the reasons why most of Stan's later films were silent, since he was all-too-aware of how easily music can compel viewers to respond in predetermined ways. In one class he projected the famed muddy battlefield sequence in Welles' *Chimes at Midnight* with the sound turned off, while in another class he did the same thing with the closing 15 minutes of Welles' *Touch of Evil*. What was fascinating was how the former film suffered heavily from that lack of sound and music, while the climactic sequence in "Touch of Evil" looked even better without any soundtrack. It was an ingenious way to make his point about the effects of music in cinema, whether for good or ill.

That attitude towards manipulation wasn't simply a shock to my cinematic sensibilities, but my attitudes towards life generally, and ignited a lifelong struggle for me with the entire notion of beauty—its purpose, its importance, and its effects on the mind. I know full well that our souls can be nurtured and healed by beauty, whether through art, nature, or our encounters with others. But I also know that beauty can hypnotize and anesthetize, and lull one into unconsciousness quite like a drug. I should know; I've been manipulated by beauty most of my life, in both constructive and destructive ways, from my creative projects and moments in nature, even to my relationships.

In the end, it left me wondering whether the purpose of art is to provide pleasure or to challenge and wake us up? Or both? It led me to scrutinize *any* situation in life that affected me strongly, whether that be an advertisement, a political debate, or simply an attractive stranger passing by me on the street. Stan once remarked how he always read at least three different biographies at the same time, never just one. When I asked him why, he said it was too easy getting caught up in someone else's life and personality; their stories and personalities tend to take over your mind, he claimed, and can influence your thoughts to the point where you start to lose yourself. Reading multiple biographies gave him more distance, more freedom, he said. It was for much the same reason, I gather, that he didn't do drugs, saying (in as many words) that he wanted to experience life without those filters. Comments like that intrigued me, and made me more aware of how the world affected me in ways I hadn't thought about before.

The Interviews

For quite a few years after graduating from college I continued sneaking into his classes whenever possible, in order to continue absorbing whatever insights he had to offer, while also looking for chances to speak with him one-on-one. Though he was always friendly, he could be cranky sometimes, but never mean-spirited. We eventually struck up a correspondence by mail, and later by phone. I appreciated the opportunity to pick his brain on a variety of topics, and in 1980 approached him with the idea of doing a series of interviews, in the hope of turning them into a book at some point down the road. To my delight, he agreed to the idea, and we met on four occasions in his hotel room at the Palmer House.

Stan Brakhage, Chicago, 1981

During those conversations we talked about his philosophy of art, literature, and film, along with a generous helping of personal anecdotes from his years working in the industry. One of those stories involved the time he was presented with a lifetime achievement award at a film festival where famed director John Ford was also slated to be honored. Brakhage received his award first, and after the hand-over was complete, the host turned to Ford and introduced the elder master with a comment about having achieved his art "without the use of tricks or special effects"—a not-so-subtle dig at Brakhage. Having spent his entire career working with little more than a camera and an editing table, Stan was mortified. "No tricks or special effects?", he said incredulously. *"What do you call a multimillion dollar studio?"*

During those conversations and in classes through the years, he expressed a certain skepticism about anything paranormal or metaphysical; yet I always had the impression there was more than met the eye to those offhand comments. That's because every now and then little clues slipped through the cracks which suggested he had more experience with moments of "high strangeness" than he really cared to admit.

One example was his story about fellow filmmaker Kenneth Anger, who not only enjoyed a certain notoriety in film circles as a pioneering talent and chronicler of Hollywood's dark underbelly in books like *Hollywood Babylon*, but also was an influential practitioner of magic—the occult sort, not the sawing-women-in-half-on-stage kind. As Stan related the story, he expressed some interest in what Kenneth and his friends were up to, so Kenneth and a few of those friends decided to instruct Stan into the basics of what they did. But Kenneth made it clear to Stan: if you really want to look into this, you need to be serious about it and not go into it halfway, since this isn't child's play. "So once the evening is over, you'll need to decide one way or another," he explained. Stan agreed.

Per their arrangement, Stan arrived at Kenneth's house and sat down with him and the others around the kitchen table, as Kenneth began explaining exactly what they did, and the basic principles involved. Shortly after that started, however, the doorbell rang and in wandered another of Kenneth's friends, someone with no involvement in their magical group, thereby interrupting this highly confidential conversation. The man sat down on one of the chairs, and began talking about some completely unrelated topic—at which point Kenneth calmly walked over to the stove behind the uninvited newcomer and turned on one of its burners with one hand while making a mysterious hand gesture in the air with the other. At exactly that moment, the guest fell unconscious in mid-sentence, his head drooping low—and remained that way until the group's talk ended. It was only then, after the group had finished saying everything they wanted to say to Stan, that Anger walked back to the stove, turned off the burner while making another hand gesture, at which point the guest lifted his head and resumed talking exactly where he left off in mid-sentence, completely clueless about what had just transpired. Stan related the anecdote without further comment.

Around 1984 my contact with him gradually tapered off. I would sometimes call him on the phone or catch up with him at a film screening he was hosting in Chicago. I also continued to notice his influence on the film industry, as his stylistic innovations begn filtering into mainstream films like Oliver Stone's *JFK* or Julien Schnabel's *Diving Bell and the Butterfly*. A couple former students of his from Colorado went on to create a hugely popular animated TV series called "South Park," and even gave Stan a bit part in a live-action film they did early on.

It was in 2003 that I received news that he'd died, at the too-young age of 69. Apparently, his exposure to various toxic chemicals from working with film stocks had taken its toll. In memory of the fallen artist, the Princeton film historian P. Adams Sitney penned these words:

> He was a painter or poet in cinema, not a novelist like everybody else. In the entire history of the medium, when all the pop-culture interests have faded, a hundred years from now, he will be considered the preeminent artist of the 20th century. [1]

Jane

His death prompted me to get back in touch with his ex-wife Jane, who I came to know over the phone during my calls out to Stan years earlier. I learned she had divorced him years earlier and changed her last name to Wodening. She was closely involved with (and starred in) many of his early films. While married to Stan, she suffered much the same fate that many wives of famous artists endure, which was to find herself sometimes relegated to the shadows of a more famous partner. Yet she had an extraordinary creative vision all her own, and through the years became a for-midable writer in her own right. (She was also born on the same day, year, and hour as singer Buddy Holly, I discovered.) Over the course of our conversations she shared stories about her years mar-ried to Stan—some of which touched yet again on that element of "high strangeness."

Still image from a video of a talk she delivered on March 8th, 2020 to the L.A. Film Forum, at an event titled "An Evening with Jane Wodening," (https://www.youtube.com/watch?v=P844IAg8rUM&feature=youtu.be)

One of those involved what seemed to be the ghost of a child who they came to call "Fred," and who seemed to tinker with a guitar in their home at odd hours. Another involved an incident she casually referred to as "the three dresses." I asked her to elab-orate. "Well, the kids were pretty little, and we had been in Lump Gulch (Colorado) for just a few years by that point. They were starting to go to school, but they were still quite little. Anyway, we were poor at the time, *really* poor, and that lasted for a few years, until Stan got that job in Chicago teaching at the School of the Art Institute. And it seems to me that when he got that job in Chicago, the money started coming in. But the magic? Not so much. And that's an interesting thing, because the 'three dresses' had to do with…poverty." I wasn't quite sure what she meant by "magic," or what that had to do with poverty—although I wondered if it related to the synchronistic way things sometimes seem to fall into place during times of urgency or even desperation. I asked her to explain.

"Well, we were thinking of taking the kids to some kind of special occasion—I don't remember what it was exactly now. But we needed the three girls to have dresses for that occasion. And all I had were casual clothes for them, you know. And I was thinking how I wasn't good at sewing back then. I still find that making a dress is terrifying! So we were wondering what to do. We couldn't buy dresses, because they were too expensive. So I was driving down the road, and Stan was in the passenger seat, when suddenly he said, 'Stop the car!' He'd seen something, obviously. We got out of the car—and right there, draped on a bush right alongside the road, were three hand-made dresses. *And each one of them was the right size for each of the three girls.* How did they wind up there? I have no idea. No idea at all."

Most surprising to me, though, was learning that Stan had actually converted back to Christianity shortly before his death. He'd always hinted at being agnostic, if not actually atheistic, during classes and conversations; yet after his divorce from Jane and starting up a new family, he apparently underwent a religious conversion and climbed back into the loving arms of the church. When Jane realized how startled I was to hear this, she remarked, "Well, Stan actually sang in the choir as a young child, he was a boy tenor, so actually he was just going back to his earliest roots." It just goes to show that you just never know.

Re-Vision

As a result of teachers like both Stan and John, a shift had taken place in my visual sensibility, not just about movies but about virtually everything else in my field of vision. The camera lens had become a magical instrument of discovery for me, an enchanted eyeglass through which to see my world from entirely new perspectives. Though I eventually stopped shooting movie footage, I became heavily involved with photography years later and found myself incorporating much of what I learned from those filmmaking years, especially in terms of trusting my intuition, learning from "accidents," and looking at scenes from unconventional angles.

I was also inspired by Stan's fiercely independent attitude towards his creativity, and how uncompromising he was in following the voice of his muse—despite all the trade-offs that entailed in terms of either income or popularity. That was a trait share by Kriyananda and Shelly as well, actually, both of whom pursued their spiritual callings without the slightest regard for what was or wasn't fashionable or considered "respectable" by their peers at the time.

As for Brakhage's legacy, there's no telling whether P. Adams Sitney's prediction will ultimately prove true; all I can really speak to is the legacy he left me. He opened my own eyes just a little bit further, and prompted me to look at things differently, and I'm grateful for that. [2]

Postscript: This is the last painting I completed before leaving art behind and shifting my attention to writing. Painted in 1978, it's a portrait of my grand-aunt Halla Guldbrandsen in Norway, shortly before her 100th birthday. An aristocratic but kind-hearted figure, when younger she had known the likes of painter Edvard Munch and the controversial writer Knut Hamsun.

CHAPTER 4

ANOMALIES

S hortly after the turn of the millennium. My friend Tim Boyd asked me if I would give a talk about Egypt to a small study group of his on the south side of Chicago. I took the train from the western suburbs into the city and then down to the south side, where I described some of my experiences in Egypt, showing some of my photographs from that region, and addressing some of the mysteries surrounding that culture.

The question invariably comes up during such gatherings about the supposed "curse" associated with the opening of Tutankhamun's tomb. It's a complicated topic but an interesting one. Among the unusual deaths following the opening of that tomb, I explained, was a fellow named Richard Bethell, the personal secretary to Howard Carter, the chief discoverer of Tut's tomb. Bethell was found dead in his bed one day, suffocated with a pillow; then, his father, Lord Westbury, fell to his death from a seventh floor window. Different theories have been suggested to explain those deaths (including one proposing they were actually murdered by none other than Aleister Crowley). But to date they remain unexplained.

After the talk was over, I got back on the train with my photographs and my notes and headed back to the western suburbs. But upon arriving home, I realized I had left my photographs on the train; the envelope they were in had slipped out of my satchel and slid off to the side of the seat. Since they were expensive, high-quality prints, I was upset, and made a point of calling the railroad's lost-and-found office the next morning to find out if they had been turned in by someone. To my relief, they had, and later that day I headed back downtown on the train to retrieve my photos.

On reaching the lost-and-found office, I was greeted by a young-ish man behind the window who said to me, while handing over the folder with my photos, "By the way, I saw your photos, and they were really interesting. I have a family connection to Egypt, you know." Oh, really? What is that? "A couple relatives of mine who were involved with the King Tut discovery died mysterious deaths." At that, I looked down at the young clerk's I.D. badge, and saw that his last name was *Bethell*. As it turned out, he was directly related to Richard Bethell, the aforementioned secretary to Howard Carter, and to Richard's father, Lord Westbury—the same figures I had just spoken about on the south side of the city. If I hadn't misplaced my batch of photos on the train that day, I would never have met him.

I've always been fascinated by odd and unusual experiences like that, by phenomena or coincidences that didn't quite fit into ordinary notions of reality. Part of that was simply because of their "entertainment" value, I suppose, since strange events broke up the routine order and mixed things up in unique and thought-provoking ways. In a word, they were *different*.

But there was always something far more to it than just that for me. For me, these experiences hinted at truths about life very different from what I'd learned from textbooks, TV, or for that matter parochial grade school. Anomalies can be paradigm-shifting, and serve as haunting reminders of life's mysteriousness, prompting us to peer just a little bit further behind that cloudy veil of appearances. I've had quite a few such encounters with anomalies over the years; what follows are a few of those that stand out most vividly for me, and that prompted me to look more closely behind that veil for myself.

⚒

One afternoon when I was 11, I was sitting in the kitchen with my mother when she stopped dead in her tracks and exclaimed, with a sense of urgency, "Something's wrong. . ." My dad was working downtown on a construction site at the time, but my mom claimed she heard him cry out her name, as if in pain. She quickly set about trying to find out what happened, but wasn't able to get through to him. She paced furiously for the next 30 minutes, worried to death about his condition. It was roughly a half-hour later that the phone rang; it was a call from a doctor's office downtown. My dad wanted to let her know that he'd been injured on the site— and it happened right at the time she heard his voice. The injury wasn't deadly serious, fortunately; he'd stepped on a nail and it went all the way through his foot. Painful as that was, it didn't become infected so he was able to return to work within a few weeks. But I'll never forget my mother's behavior that day, and how she seemed to know something was wrong with my father.

When I was 12, I saw a segment on TV about an opera singer who could supposedly shatter a wine glass using only her voice. (This wasn't the famous recording tape commercial some readers may be familiar with that appeared on TV some years later.) That so intrigued me that the next evening I got it in my head to attempt this feat on my own, using a crystal bowl on our dining room table as my target. I sat down in a room adjacent to the dining room, roughly twelve feet away, and began letting out a high-pitch "EEEEE!," all the while focusing my attention *intently* on that crystal bowl.

My parents wondered what I was doing, but they were so used to me doing odd things by then that they paid little attention after the first few seconds. I let out my ear-piercing screech several more times—when on the fifth or sixth try, the crystal bowl on the table shattered and collapsed into pieces across the dining room table. Though I had secretly hoped that would happen, I was nonetheless surprised it actually did. The sound of the bowl splitting apart on the wooden table made enough noise that my mother rushed in from the kitchen and asked, "*What in the world happened?*" When I explained to her how I shattered the bowl using my voice, she was incredulous. But she could see I wasn't anywhere near the bowl, so she didn't quite know what to make of it, and examined the glass pieces hoping to find some clues as to what really happened. Years later I mentioned the incident to a sound engineer; like my mother, he was skeptical as well, saying that the notion of shattering glass with one's voice is more of a myth than reality. Yet it did happen—or rather, *something* happened. Was it a "paranormal" event? Maybe not, but it certainly wasn't normal.

It's no doubt significant that most of the anomalous events I've experienced in life occurred for me roughly between the ages of 10 and 16. As all students of the anomalous and the paranormal know, that's often the case, and possibly related to the fact this period also happens to be ground zero for puberty, when our vital energies reach a bursting point and may well overflow into externalized manifestations and synchronicities of one sort or another. For me, that's included numerous sightings of unusual lights in the sky. As for one example, I was about 13 when I happened to look out the window from an upstairs bedroom in our house one afternoon and saw a strange set of lights off towards the Eastern horizon. They looked to be over the city of Chicago, connected to one another, and were cruising slowly from south on my right to north on my left. I grabbed the set of binoculars I'd just received for my birthday and focused on the image more closely. What I saw were two rows of very bright lights, one atop the other, looking almost like passenger windows from a jet airliner, lit up from inside. Except this was the middle of the day, a time when one normally can't see lights inside of a jet cabin. Plus, I distinctly saw *two* rows of lights, one atop the other, not just one.

The craft—or whatever it was—continued on its slow northward drift until it finally disappeared from view somewhere north of the city. The next day, I combed the newspaper to see if there was any mention of this event—and was pleasantly surprised to see there was. In a small article on the front page of our main Chicago paper was a story about reports from around the area of an unusual craft with two rows of lights seen cruising over the city, moving slowly from south to north, exactly at the time when I had my own sighting. There was never any further explanation or suggestion as to what those lights might have been, and I imagine the incident was completely forgotten by everyone except me.

It was around that same period I was sitting in the kitchen of our house talking with my mother about her own mother, my grandmother, who passed away a year earlier. In the midst of reminiscing about her mother, we heard a loud "klanging" noise coming from the basement. That was wholly unexpected, and we went downstairs to investigate. There, in the middle of the basement floor, was a metal dinner tray—the same one my grandmother used to eat food on during her final years living with us. It had been lying flat up on a shelf, and not positioned in such a way that any slight movement would have likely knocked it off. (A mouse certainly couldn't have done it.) Try as we might, we couldn't determine how that tray would have been dislodged and knocked to the floor. Not surprisingly, my mother took it as a sign of acknowledgement from her late mother, especially considering the timing of when it happened.

During my college years I agreed to help a classmate named Alan do some painting in the old house on the north side of Chicago that he was renting. That first day, he was off in the back of the house painting one room while I was painting an empty closet in the front of the house, when I suddenly felt someone touch my shoulder. I turned around expecting to see my friend, Alan—but to my surprise, no one was there. I chalked it up to a case of a random muscle twitching and continued painting. Then, ten minutes later, I felt the same sensation on my shoulder again, but this time it was more forceful and distinct. There was no mistaking it: someone was definitely touching me. But like before, I turned around to find no one was there. I was beginning to feel a bit rattled at this point, but my friend was a down-to-earth type who didn't believe in anything he couldn't touch or see, so I decided to be cautious and not say anything to him about my experience.

Several weeks later, I was surprised when Alan confided to me in guarded tones that he thought his house was "haunted." When I asked him why, he cautiously began describing a series of bizarre experiences he had at the house, all considerably more dramatic than my own. They began with the sound of playful laughing whenever he would undress, then climaxed late one night when his bed started shaking, awakening him abruptly. It was almost like an earthquake, he said, except nothing else in the room was shaking. He quickly climbed out of bed—at which point he found himself pushed up against the bedroom wall, as if by unseen hands. "It scared the living shit out of me," he said. When I told him about my own experience two weeks earlier, he seemed relieved to hear he wasn't the only one who experienced strange things there.

As it turned out, both of us knew a young woman at our school—Debby, the same one who first exposed me to the Hermetic axiom "As above, so below," in fact—who said she knew a psychic our own age named Jim, who might be able to do a "clearing" of sorts in the house. So she arranged to bring him to the house one afternoon to see what he could pick up. Though Alan said nothing to Jim about his own experience beforehand, Jim walked through the house and claimed to pick up impressions of a female spirit—one who had grown quite fond of Alan, in fact, and who was basically being mischievous. Jim did a ritual cleaning intended to send the spirit on its way. Did it work? All I know is my friend Al never had any problem with those disturbances again.

⇥ ⇤

During the early 1970s while studying at the Art Institute of Chicago, I became close friends with a fellow film student by the name of Bill Hogan. Early in 1972, he hatched a plan for us to shoot some footage along the coast of California for an experimental film he was working on, and I thought to myself this might be a good chance for me to capture some footage as well. We even managed to convince our one instructor John Schofill to join up and drive all of us to the coast in his car during spring break. He'd lived in California before moving to Chicago, where he organized film screenings on the Berkeley campus, and saw this as a chance to go back and visit old friends there. So on April Fool's Day of that year, John, Bill and his girlfriend Debbie, and myself set out from the slushy, snowy Chicagoland area for the sunny seeming utopia of California.

We spent a little over a week exploring the Bay area, including San Francisco, Mill Valley, and Berkeley, as well as several days around Big Sur. I'd been to California once before during a family trip when I was twelve, but this was an altogether different adventure. This time, I felt like Dorothy stepping from her black and white world into that other one of stunning technicolor. There literally seemed to be different hues in the environment from anything I was familiar with back home; the skies seemed bluer, the violet blossoms of the Jacaranda trees around Berkeley had an ethereal quality, and there seemed to be an energy in the air which I found intoxicating.

The week we spent out there opened my mind in any number of ways, and some of that due to the hallucinogenic experiences we had during that time. The first of those was in the otherworldly landscape of Big Sur. John dropped Bill and I off at the nearby campground there, where we stayed and shot film for several days while John went off to visit old friends around the Bay area. Several days earlier, we caught wind of the fact that one of John's friends had access to some supposedly pure LSD, and we managed to convince him to give us some. Bill and I brought it along, and we ingested one dose each at the Big Sur campground, then set off on foot down the long and winding road to Pfeiffer Beach, overlooking the Pacific Ocean. I had no idea what that route looked like beforehand. As the drug began taking effect, the journey down that road took on quasi-mythic proportions for me. The landscape evolved and transformed in astonishing ways, and after what seemed like an eternity, we finally emerged from out of the tangle of trees and sand onto Pfeiffer Beach itself—a staggering natural site which harbors a mystical ambience that can't really be put into words, nor should it be.

But as powerful as that experience was, an even more mind-altering one unfolded for me several days later when the five of us traveled to Mills College and situated ourselves in a beautiful natural area behind the college proper. This spot struck me as kind of a well-tended swamp, or what some call a "wetland." Thick with fauna and vegetation, I found it idyllic in a lush sort of way. On arriving there, Bill and I ingested our remaining LSD, but in a slightly larger dosages this time, and the results were transformative.

My perception of the world became profoundly synchronistic, as I began to notice how everything around me—sounds, feelings, images, actions—seemed to be interwoven within a larger, cosmic symphony of meaning. Several years later I read Andrew Weil's book *The Natural Mind* and was struck by a phrase he used in connection with an experience reported by users of hallucinogens in the Bay area during the 60s—"positive paranoia." Simply, that's a sense that *everything happening around you is a conspiracy for your benefit.* In many cases, no doubt, that perception is little more than a drug-induced fantasy. But there are times, whether drug-induced or otherwise, when it seems unmistakably real. For me, this was one of those—and it would become one of the early experiences that eventually fueled my later studies with synchronicity.

As the minutes rolled on, it felt as though the psychic barriers armoring my perception dissolved and allowed me to intuitively tune into the emotions of everyone—and everything—around me. While talking to Bill, I somehow knew what he was going to say before he said it. As surprising as that was, there was an even greater shock awaiting me, as I explored the fauna and flora of the surrounding garden. I gradually began to sense faint sounds coming from a long row of nearby bushes and flowers. They weren't audible in any normal sense, but were more like "feeling-impressions" of sounds, for lack of a better description. At one point it finally dawned on me that the sounds were originating from the *plants themselves*—and they were consciously communicating with me.

With that moment of shocked recognition on my part, a ripple of laughter peeled through the rows of plants, as if they were aware of my surprise and even *delighted* in it. It reminded me of yet another iconic scene from the *Wizard of Oz*, when Dorothy hears the tittering noises coming from the plants when she entered that technicolor world. Over the next hour—though for all I know it could have been just ten minutes—I proceeded to communicate with the plants, or at least believed I was, as I projected different emotions outward towards the plants and they responded collectively as if in response.

After returning home from that trip, I was determined to find comparisons to other, more familiar sounds they could be likened to, and eventually settled on Ravel's composition "Daphnes and Chloe, Suite 2," with its opening bars of rippling, cascading notes. That intro expressed much the same quality as what I heard that day, except what I experienced that day were more natural and organic sounds than anything created through human-made orchestral instruments.

Despite how vivid and "real" all this felt to me, I naturally had nagging doubts. I wanted an informed second opinion, so several years later asked Goswami Kriyananda for his thoughts on what I'd experienced. On hearing my detailed description, he responded quite matter-of-factly, "Oh sure, it was real, but it was very *limited*." What do you mean by "limited," I wondered? "You see, *everything* is conscious," he said. "But your awareness opened up only far enough to pick up the consciousness of the plants. Had it opened up farther, you would have been able to sense the awareness of the rocks, the clouds, the trees—*everything*."

(Curiously enough, several years later Kriyananda described an experience of his own that was similar to mine, but even stranger. While coming out of a deep meditation one day, he opened his eyes to see his dog lying on the floor chewing on a bone. But to his surprise, he sensed a consciousness stirring in the bone which expressed itself essentially as, "It's so nice to be enjoyed!" The bone not only possessed a rudimentary awareness, in other words, but appreciated being devoured by the hungry dog. That came as a shock to Kriyananda, a down-to-Earth double-Taurus who never even considered the possibility something as inanimate or seemingly "dead" as a bone could be conscious, let alone that it might derive pleasure from being consumed.)

There have been times in my life when I entered a new environment for the first time and seemed able to pick up impressions which were accurate about that place and its history. One of those occurred for me during the early 70's while staying at the summer cottage of my childhood friend Kirk during the early 1970s. I'd driven up from Illinois across the border into Wisconsin to spend the day with him, and when it came time to retire for the evening, I headed off to the side bedroom to sleep for the night.

While lying in bed, though, I was surprised by the wave of peculiar images I saw floating through my mind. I was completely sober, yet it felt as though I'd taken a hallucinogenic drug, the colors and forms were so vivid and surrealistic. Even more surprising was how *foreign* all this mental pageantry seemed to me, as though it had erupted from someone else's imagination. The ideas and environments were different from anything I was familiar with from my own dreams and hypnagogic reveries. Even the faces on the people flashing by seemed new and different somehow. It went on like this for well over an hour, until I finally fell asleep.

The next morning over breakfast I mentioned that to my friend, who laughed when he heard it. When I asked what was so funny, he said, "That's the bed I used to lie in whenever I did LSD or mescaline back in the old days. I must have done 40 or 50 trips lying on that bed in that room." It was hard not to think I might have been immersed in a veritable cloud of residual thought forms and fantasies lying there that warm summer night, all of them likely "borrowed" from the mind of another.

That wasn't the only time I had a sense of an environment and its impressions. The year was 1982 and I was getting ready to embark on my first trip to England, and had been contemplating the places I hoped to visit while there. I'd read a bit about the history of the Battle of Hastings in 1066, when William the Conqueror came ashore with his army of Normans and overthrew the reigning king of England. Something about that historical episode called to me, and I started thinking about visiting the site of that historical battle.

One week before I was set to leave on my trip, I was standing in line at the bank ready to withdraw some money, when my thoughts turned to this possible destination and whether I should make a side-trip to Hastings to explore it. Exactly at that moment, I happened to notice the fellow standing in line in front of me; he was scratching the back of his head and had a check in his hand, apparently intending to cash or deposit it. The number of the address printed on that check? *1066.* That was surprising enough, but then I saw the fellow's name on the check: *Norman Wave.* That settled it: I included Hastings in my itinerary.

Once there, I walked around the battlefield, which struck me as unusually peaceful in a pastoral sort of way. Nothing particularly stood out for me, however, and I eventually made my way over by bus to the ocean, where I wandered along the beach and climbed amongst the ruins of an ancient structure constructed by William the Conqueror after settling in as England's new monarch. I had been up most of the previous night, and at one point decided to lie down and rest, at which point I drifted in and out of sleep. It was then, on that ethereal threshold between waking and sleep, that I heard a deep-throated, guttural voice in my head saying, clear as a bell: "...*fear of Saxon power*." That immediately woke me, since it was so distinct. Was I picking up on impressions that locals in the area felt centuries earlier about the impending arrival of William's army? I have no way of knowing. All I can say for sure is the voice was unlike any I'd heard before.

⋙╫⋘

Nine years later I was living with my wife in the western suburbs of Chicago, in a tiny house in the woods. (And I do mean *tiny*: the foundation of the house measured 11 x 22 feet, complete.) This was during the mid-1990s, and late one night I laid there in bed next to her, mulling over some problems I'd been experiencing at work that week. She had fallen asleep, but I was restless, and tossed and turned on the futon mattress we were sleeping on for several hours. At one point I heard the distinct sound of heavy footsteps walking across the floor from the back of the small house and proceeding directly to the side of the bed where I was lying. The sounds of the steps finally stopped just inches from my head. Whoever this person was, I thought, they must be large and were wearing heavy boots, judging from the heavy *klop, klop, klop* of the steps.

I was petrified. I knew I had locked the one door into our small house, I assumed this stranger must have broken in somehow, and likely didn't have our best interests at heart. I was at a complete loss for what to do, since I was in a helpless position with this stranger now standing directly over me. (Was he holding an axe? A gun? My imagination went wild.) For lack of a better strategy, I decided to play possum and simply lie there motionless until the stranger started walking away, at which point I could possibly devise some further plan.

Yet to my surprise, there were no more sounds, no further "walking away" of the footsteps. After about fifteen very tense minutes of lying there perfectly still, I finally opened my eyes and peeked upward to see where the unwelcome intruder was— only to discover no one was there at all. I got up and carefully searched the small house, went to check the front door and found that it was still locked. How was that possible? The next morning I told Judith about the incident, and she mentioned how on one other occasion she had the same experience, with the sound of the heavy boots moving across the room. It was also around that time she learned that the previous tenant in that small house had been an eccentric fellow who lived there by himself for decades, and wore heavy boots much of the time because of the damp ground in the surrounding woods, where he would walk out every week to shoot squirrels and birds with his shotgun.

⟻╬╀⟼

There were other unusual experiences associated with that house during those years. Through an odd chain of circumstances, I crossed paths during the early 1990s with a fellow named Tom Stultz, who lived in a nearby suburb and served as current president of the Illinois chapter of MUFON—the Mutual UFO Network. A diminutive man in his 60s, I became friends with him and his wife, Judy. We originally connected because of a man I'd come across months earlier who had been an eyewitness at Roswell in 1947 (which in turn led to Tom linking me up with UFO researcher Stanton Friedman). Tom was a treasure trove of information on the subject, and would occasionally show me some interesting artifact or piece of footage on videotape that had never been made public before. He eventually invited me on a few occasions to attend some of their monthly MUFON meetings, and while I never became a formal member of the group, I found the conversations stimulating, since the members were well-educated, and included a research chemist, a computer specialist, and a psychologist, among others. These were definitely not garden variety weirdos.

At one point Tom asked if I'd like to come with Judith to a MUFON meeting which he cryptically suggested might be a bit "out of the ordinary." That intrigued me. We drove to his house in nearby Downers Grove on the appointed evening, at which point we learned that the speaker that night would be talking about UFOs—with the added detail that the man supposedly had an ability to communicate with alien intelligences. Judith and I looked at each other warily, not sure how to respond to that. Tom didn't necessarily believe the young man's claim himself, but said he'd heard some intriguing things about the man from a couple of his colleagues, and thought it was worth at least giving him a chance to demonstrate his supposed talents.

The young man had a thick notebook crammed with elaborate drawings of various alien races—extraterrestrials, ultra-terrestrials, para-terrestrials, and so on. At the very least, it was clear he was neck-deep into this subject. We all sat in a circle, and once the meeting was formally underway, the lights were turned down and he made some introductory comments, leading the group in a brief meditation. He then asked all of us if we had any questions for our unseen alien guests (who he seemed to imply were high above the Earth in their crafts, monitoring the group in some way.)

As skeptical as Judith and I were, we joined in on the proceedings by posing our own questions. When Judith's turn came around, she played the doubting Thomas by asking the unseen intelligences to provide some sort of proof that they actually existed and weren't just figments of the young man's imagination. "Anytime during the evening, if you could provide some evidence of your presence, that would be fine," she added. The man's response was affirmative, saying, "Okay, we'll see what we can do." When we left Tom's home that night, Judith and I confided to each other how far-fetched this had seemed, and proceeded to put the events of the evening out of our minds.

Later that night at home, several minutes after I went to bed and fell asleep Judith remained awake, sitting on the edge of our bed going through the day's mail. Then, as she described it to me the next morning, a basketball-sized sphere of light suddenly appeared outside one of the windows of our small house. As she described it, it floated into the house *through* the window, but without breaking the glass. As it then glided slowly in her direction, she tried to awaken me, but I didn't respond—which in itself was odd since I'm an extremely light sleeper. To her shock, the glowing sphere floated right up to her face—then exploded noiselessly in a flash of light, leaving no trace of any kind. As startling as all of that was, she inexplicably reclined back and went right to sleep, making no further effort to awaken me or reflect on this bizarre incident. It was almost as though she had been in a trance throughout the experience.

The next morning when she told me what happened, I didn't know what to think. But when I reminded her of the challenge she posed to the supposed "aliens" that previous evening, she turned pale, because it was only then that she started connecting the dots. She was excited, but also confused about what to make of it all. She decided to call up Tom and tell him what happened. Before she was halfway through her story, he quickly interjected, "Let me guess—you saw a ball of light, right?" She asked how he could have possibly known that, to which he responded, "Well, that seems to be the way it works around this fellow."

To this day I don't know what to make of what happened that night. But it occurred to me later on how much the gathering that night seemed to resemble a séance in some respects, considering how the participants were arranged in a circle and the young man opened up with an "invocation" of sorts. Did the group conjure something up that night? Possibly. But it may well have been something quite different from "aliens."

All of which brings me back to the central question: *What do these experiences mean?* In the next chapter I present some ideas about a more symbolic and synchronistic approach toward unlocking that mystery. As I hope will become clear, it's not really possible to separate happenings like these from the consciousness or even destinies of those experiencing them.

CHAPTER 5

PORTALS OF STRANGENESS
OR, WHAT DOES IT MEAN WHEN WEIRD
THINGS HAPPEN?

I was just thirteen at the time, sitting with a friend on the front
porch of his home, talking about the sort of things 13-year-olds
normally talk about, when I noticed an odd light in the distance
out of the corner of my eye. He noticed it, too, and we turned
our heads to see a brightly glowing disc rising up over the trees,
probably a half-mile away. It was shaped like the top half of a ham-
burger bun, I thought to myself, and was cream-colored, with a

strange iridescent green along its fringe. After rising up a short distance, the disc darted around in a strange, jerky way, unlike any airplane or hot air balloon I'd ever seen, before moving off into the distance and dropping out of view beneath the tree line. The entire experience lasted maybe 40 seconds in all.

We were stunned by what we'd witnessed, since it was so different from anything we'd encountered before, outside of Hollywood movies, that is. I'd seen those strange lights off in the distance over Chicago several months earlier, but this was much closer, and much clearer. When we tried describing what we saw to our parents, our stories were brushed off as the products of overactive imaginations. I even tried calling up the nearby airport to report what we saw to find out if anyone else reported it, but they dismissed my story as simple misidentification. "Oh, that was just a blimp with advertising lights on it," he assured me patronizingly, adding how there was one in the area that day. I said no, we'd actually seen the blimp he was talking about, roughly 45 minutes earlier, and it was completely different from what we saw. But he wasn't convinced. "No, that was just a blimp you saw. But thanks for calling"—click.

We've probably all had brushes at one point or another with events that baffle us, even if that was just an unlikely coincidence or a hunch that turned out to be accurate. But what about the *truly* odd event—like a peculiar craft darting around in the sky? Or a rainfall of frogs from the sky, like my friend Paul Mahalek's grandmother told me she witnessed as a child back in Indiana?

The renegade researcher Charles Fort (1874-1932) spent the better part of his life collecting such stories and compiling them into books like *Lo!* and *The Book of the Damned*, in the process inspiring countless other researchers and even a magazine that commemorates his legacy, *Fortean Times*. Presuming we don't just dismiss all these strange accounts as simple hallucinations, hoaxes, or misidentifications, what are we to make of these tales?

Having studied accounts like these closely, and experienced more than a few of my own, I've come to see these events hold profound significance for those of us who experience them. There's something strangely fitting about when and where they occur—not just for the individuals themselves but sometimes even for society at large.

It naturally begs the question: Are things like ghosts, flying saucers, or Bigfoot-like creatures actually "real"? They certainly are real to those who experience them. Over the years my focus has become more phenomenological in nature, less concerned with the objective "reality" of these strange events than their role in the lives of those encountering them. What follows is an attempt to provide a framework for understanding these phenomena, as seen through the lens of synchronicity and symbolism. This involves a two-fold approach. The first is holistic, and involves studying the larger network of events constellated around these phenomena, since they always seem enmeshed within larger patterns of significance at the time.

But it also involves the critical step of asking, What do these phenomena *symbolize?* For as important as those patterns of events and webs of synchronicity are, it all means little if we don't take the added step to explore the *archetypal meanings* encoded within these events and patterns. And to do that, we need take a deep dive into the symbolic heart of these phenomena, approaching them much as we would if we were interpreting a dream. To say it another way, *Fortean phenomena are best understood as elements within an overarching symbolic worldview.*

A Synchronistic World View

First, a few definitions are in order. The Swiss psychologist Carl Jung sometimes defined *synchronicity* as an occurrence of "meaningful coincidence," involving the intersection of an outer event with an inner state of mind, or as the correspondence between two outer events. We experience many coincidences in the course of our lives, but the majority of them tend to be trivial, not in any way really meaningful. Coming across the name "Mary" twice in a day is a coincidence, but a pretty superficial one. But suppose you stumble across a photo of someone you haven't heard from in 20 years, only to have them call you on the phone at that exact moment. *That's* a synchronicity.

Over the years I've come to believe that synchronicities are best understood as fundamentally *symbolic events*. According to various mystical traditions through history, our universe can be thought of as an expression of mind-stuff, more akin to our nightly dreams than the "solid" world described by strict materialists. "Things here are signs," the ancient philosopher Plotinus said. For that reason, outer events can be interpreted in much the same way as dream images, concealing layers of symbolism beyond their surface appearances. According to this worldview, all phenomena interlock in a profound and intricate way that reflects the workings of a vast intelligence, or what the Buddhists refer to as *Big Mind*. Nothing is chance, nothing is disconnected from the whole. As such, synchronicities—isolated dramatic coincidences—are actually just the tip of a larger iceberg of meaningfulness that extends throughout our lives, and in turn, the entire cosmos.

But while all phenomena possess a certain significance, one particular kind of event has always been viewed as holding special importance, which can be summarized this way: *the more unusual an event, the greater its importance as a symbol of change.*

For example, overhearing the same number or name mentioned twice in a day may be uncommon but it's not particularly unusual. Or seeing a woman in a polka-dot dress may be out of the ordinary but it's nothing shockingly different. But seeing a dog give birth to a two-headed puppy? Now, *that's* unusual! Indeed, the ancient Babylonians made a systematic study of just such oddities as part of their long-term study of omens and symbols, in hope of extracting predictable patterns from their occurrence. The sheer unusualness of such events was taken as signaling tectonic shifts in the natural order of things.

This is where Fortean events take center stage, because they're about as unusual as it gets. Strange animals, rainfalls of frogs, time slips, glowing craft flying through the sky, divine apparitions—these rank high on life's Richter Scale of "high strangeness," and hold special significance as signposts of transformation. These are the types of events I want to focus on here.

That said, I'd like to propose viewing Fortean events on at least two distinct levels: *personal* and *collective.*

Anomalies: Personal and Collective

For those who experience them, anomalous events invariably happen during times of extraordinary change—emotionally, intellectually, or spiritually. When I experienced that odd light in the sky, I was undergoing a major change in my own life. I kept a diary at the time, so I was able to go back and see what was happening for me back then. Part of that simply involved puberty, of course, but above and beyond that it was a period of explosive new interests for me. The appearance of that disc coincided closely with a major shift taking place in my attitudes since I had just started discovering books and articles about subjects beyond rock-and-roll, monster movies, or Sci-Fi paperbacks. There was a "meaningful coincidence" between my outer and inner reality then, aptly symbolized by that strange glowing disc. To my mind, it possessed a certain futuristic quality which hinted at progressive new ideas emerging in my own life.

As an astrologer, I've consistently found that Fortean events are paralleled by important planetary configurations taking shape for individuals when the phenomena occur. Years after my incident with the glowing disc, for example, I was intrigued to look back and discover that my experience happened precisely as

Uranus was forming a powerful relationship to my horoscope—a planetary energy normally associated with surprising or even shocking new insights or experiences in life. As I'll continue to show here, understanding planetary patterns can sometimes be a useful key for teasing out the subtler inflections of anomalous events.

A Haunting

One afternoon during my high school years, I was lounging in an upstairs bedroom of our family home reading a book. I'd been up there for about a half hour, when I heard the sound of heavy footsteps slowly walking up the stairs, each one as clear as day. It was an old staircase, and whenever anyone ascended those stairs the sounds creaked all the way up from bottom to top, thirteen steps in all. That happened this time as well—but this time they climaxed in total silence.

I didn't think much about that at first, although I did expect someone to walk into my bedroom, which was located directly adjacent to the staircase. To my surprise, no one appeared. I finally got up to take a look, only to find that no one was there at all—just an empty staircase. I thought I was home alone at the time, but just to make sure I went downstairs and looked around. But there was no one else in the house at all; I was completely alone, and the sounds I heard were as distinct as could be.

In contrast to the unidentified light in the sky several years earlier, which coincided with radical new ideas entering my life, that ghostly encounter seemed to coincide more closely with problems I was struggling to *let go* of and simply *forget*. Specifically, I had just experienced an extremely painful social situation at school the day before (and is there anything more disturbing to a teenager than a painful social situation? I think not). Said another way, the apparent haunting occurred at a time when I was feeling "haunted" myself.

Now, whether that sound I heard truly *was* a "ghost" is less important, since my approach, as I mentioned, is a more phenomenological one. I *believed* it was a ghost, so within my own experiential matrix at the time it held that basic meaning. In the examples we'll be looking at here I'll be adopting much the same approach, rather than trying to judge the reality or illusoriness of the stories reported. From the symbolist standpoint, there is significance to be mined either way.

Let's turn our attention now to the broader level, and consider what these phenomena could mean for society-at-large.

The Collective Dimension

Just as anomalous events hold a synchronistic meaning for individuals, so they hold significance for communities and cultures as well, similar to dream symbols but on a far grander scale.

As I pointed out, one way of approaching any anomalous event is through studying its *context*. While our tendency is to see events in relative isolation, Carl Jung and others noted how ancient cultures like the Chinese employed a kind of "field thinking" which looked at events in groups and asked, "*What tends to happen together in time?*" Synchronistic thinking requires not only a gift for metaphor and symbolism, but an ability to think holistically, and perceive the larger patterns constellated around an event.

For example, in June 2013, an ancient Egyptian statuette on display in an English museum was found to have pivoted 180 degrees around on its base. Since no one had ever seen that happen with this exhibit before, museum officials were mystified and had no ready explanation. To help solve the mystery, they installed a surveillance camera to observe it over time in hope of finding the source of that movement. Indeed, time-lapse video showed the statuette shifting on its base very slowly over many hours, yet there was still no obvious cause for the shift. Some speculated it was the result of vibrations triggered by passing museum-goers, or a nearby transit train, while still others clung to a more paranormal explanation.

Whatever the reason, the sheer unusualness of this event invited me to consider its possible meaning. Why did this occurrence happen and become such a media sensation *right at that time?* One possibility would be to look at the larger historical context around the time it happened, to see if other events might help shed some light on it.

In fact, what we find is just this: several weeks later, Egypt underwent a profound upheaval as mounting public pressure forced the removal of its Islamic-leaning president, Mohammed Morsi. Could it be that the "about face" of that statue in the Manchester museum was somehow a portent of the political reversal about to upset Egyptian culture itself? Looked at in terms of its symbolism, that's a real possibility.

Decoding the Roswell Incident

Another iconic event in the annals of Fortean phenomena was the rumored crash of one or more alien spacecraft near Roswell, New Mexico in 1947. According to some researchers and students of the event, the craft was later retrieved by the United States military and reverse-engineered by researchers to procure whatever high-tech secrets it held.

It's important to realize first off that this wasn't the only "otherworldly" phenomenon taking place at the time. Just two weeks earlier, on June 24th, another iconic event in Fortean lore, Kenneth Arnold's sighting of flying discs in Washington State, occurred. And several days before *that*, seaman Harold Dahl claimed to have witnessed six UFOs near Maury Island in Puget Sound, Washington, and the next morning also reported what would be the first documented "Men in Black" encounter.

What does it mean that so many dramatic events centering around UFOs took place in so short a time?

Viewed as a complex of events rather than just as isolated incidents, it's safe to say that the winds of change were in the air. With their hints of advanced intelligences and superior technologies, a futuristic archetype was clearly at work, symbolically pointing to emerging new trends in the world.

And indeed, there were a number of historic shifts taking place during that period. Technology was advancing at a breakneck speed, especially in atomic weaponry and computer development; the CIA was set into motion that same month; and the United States Air Force became an independent governmental agency at the same time. (In fact, a B-25 bomber sent to investigate the Maury Island incident crashed on August 1st of that year—the very same day the United States Air Force came into being.) On a global scale, the sense of optimism that was emerging globally in the wake of WWII was coupled by a growing sense of anxiety and unpredictability in regions like China, Israel, and India (where, in the latter instance, the world's largest democracy was being born amidst great social turmoil).

An important key to unlocking what was happening that year can also be found in the astrology of that time. Precisely when all three of these Fortean incidents took place, the planet Uranus was just completing its second full circuit around the zodiac from where it was positioned on its discovery in 1781—a "Uranus return," as astrologers refer to it. Symbolically, Uranus is the planet of revolution, aviation, and innovation, so a return to its place of zodiacal origin like this clearly signals an amplification of progressive trends and paradigms in the collective arena.

Because Uranus is the planet associated with the zodiacal sign Aquarius, it's even possible that the events of that period offer a significant "window" into the emerging Aquarian Age itself— which, depending on one's perspective, could be a cause for either jubilation or concern. Were the events of 1947 portending a future of exciting new technologies, scientific breakthroughs, and even interaction with extraterrestrial intelligences? Or were those events warning us about an age of government surveillance, cover-ups, and technological complications? Or even all of the above? One way or another, it will be interesting to watch the next major return of Uranus to that discovery point—slated to take place in the 2030-2031 period.

Let's turn our attention now to one of the most iconic events in all of Fortean folklore—the filming of an alleged Bigfoot in California by Roger Patterson and Bob Gimlin on October 20th of 1967.

The Patterson-Gimlin "Bigfoot Film"

As the story goes, the two men were traveling on horseback through an area called Bluff Creek, when they spotted a large dark figure in a nearby creek bed. Patterson climbed down off his horse, grabbed the movie camera he had with him at the time, and proceeded to film the creature as it lumbered off into the woods.

To this day, the footage remains a source of heated debate, but despite repeated claims by skeptics of possible hoaxing it's important to point out no one has ever successfully reproduced the appearance of that creature on film in a convincing way. Whatever one's opinion about the footage, all parties agree that it represents a turning point in our modern fascination with this creature, and for that reason represents a synchro-Fortean event of the highest order.

Taking a purely symbolic approach to the footage, we could start by looking at it strictly in terms of its imagery, as if we were examining someone's dream symbolism. The creature in this footage is obviously wild and untamed, halfway between human and animal, straddling the threshold between civilization and nature. It's entirely naked and covered with fur, yet it stands upright and walks similar to how a human does. Its muscular figure conveys a sense of enormous power, yet at the same time it displays female breasts!

Viewed as a collective dream symbol, as it were, the appearance of this creature in 1967 can be read as signaling something primal surfacing from the "wilds" of the collective unconscious, an energy paradoxically both ancient and new. The figure embodies great power, yet its feminine gender hints at a consciousness that is more right-brain and intuitive than anything purely aggressive or animalistic. It personifies a consciousness midway between ordered civilization and untamed nature, betwixt pure rationality and raw emotional impulses.

With those points in mind, let's now adopt our Chinese "field thinking" approach and see what other socio-cultural developments were taking place around that encounter, to see if anything stands out that might illumine the symbolism I'm suggesting here. When I went back and carefully examined the historical record from that time, I came across a number of events that seemed not only relevant, but at times uncanny:

* Two days before the Patterson-Gimlin encounter, on October 18, Disney Studios released the popular animated feature *The Jungle Book*. The film's scenario revolves around a boy raised by animals in the wild, and follows his escapades as he mingles on the threshold between nature and civilization, between life in the wild and domesticated village life.

* One day before that, on October 17th, the enormously successful musical *Hair* premiered on Broadway. This long-running production was embraced by fans as a celebration of personal freedom and Dionysian self-expression, but was derided by some conservative critics as promoting amorality and regressive values. The musical's title itself hints at how the hippies at the show's core shunned the neatly groomed fashions of mainstream society in favor of wilder, more natural looks. The musical became especially controversial for

a scene in which all the cast members appeared on stage fully naked.

* Less than a week earlier, on October 12th, Desmond Morris's bestselling book *The Naked Ape* was released, a popularized attempt to frame human nature in the context of Darwinian evolution. It suggested that we need to view humans as just one animal species among many, and tried to explain our behaviors in light of those exhibited by our mammalian kin. The book's title came from the fact that out of 193 species of monkey and apes, humans are the only ones not fully covered in hair.

* Three weeks after the Patterson-Gimlin encounter, the Bible of the rock-and roll counterculture, *Rolling Stone*, premiered. (November 9th was the cover date on the first issue, but as is common practice in the publishing industry, it appeared on newsstands earlier.) Contrasted with publications like the ultra-conservative Wall Street Journal with that paper's embrace of short haircuts, business suits, and "square" values, Rolling Stone celebrated much the same ideals as the musical "Hair": alternate lifestyles, long hair, music, and Dionysian self-expression. Though it spawned many imitators through the years, it remains an influential magazine to this day.

* The human/primate interface was a surprisingly popular meme in all the arts throughout this period. Several months after the P-G incident, on February 8th, 1968, the first in the hugely successful *Planet of the Apes* film franchise premiered, centering around a society of unusually intelligent apes; while 1967 saw the peak popularity of the TV show *The Monkees*, showcasing a group of long-haired Beatle imitators (and whose records actually outsold both the Beatles and the Rolling Stones that year), with episodes frequently picturing the actors alongside images of actual or stuffed monkeys.

* Another way that the counter-cultural impulses of the
period were making their presence felt was through the
burgeoning protest movement, with ordinary citizens ral-
lying to express their anger over governmental policies—a
development some commentators described as "the awakening of a sleeping giant." In light of that, it's worth noting that one day after the Patterson-Gimlin encounter, a
historic march in Washington, D.C. took place, with tens of
thousands of citizens lining the streets of the nation's capi-
tal to protest America's involvement in the Vietnam War.
As clearly as any other event from that period, that march
embodied the grassroots energies of the 60's coming to the
surface in a dramatic way.

Putting all of these pieces together, the picture that starts emerging is indeed one of a powerful force welling up in the collective
psyche—a force simultaneously rooted in the intuitive-emotional
aspects of our nature as well as our more rational faculties. (After
all, developments like *Hair, The Jungle Book, Rolling Stone,* and the
march in Washington weren't simply expressions of Dionysian
abandon and unbridled anarchy; in each case, their execution all
involved considerable forethought and intelligence.)

Just consider the 1960's, and all the countercultural forces that
were coming to light at the time: people were shedding their conservative fashions and adopting wilder, more uninhibited appearances. The Back-To-Nature movement was on the rise, with 1967
ushering in the "Summer of Love" and "Flower Power." The Beatles
released "Sergeant Pepper" that year. There was a general sense of
heightened creativity in the air, as people from various walks of
life woke up to the possibility of becoming forces for change in the
world, whether as grass-roots activists or celebrities and rock stars.

Yet alongside all this was a palpable sense of danger and potential violence, as all those pent-up energies were being unleashed,

something reflected not just in protest movements, big city riots, or bombings, but even in the arts. One month before the Patterson-Gimlin encounter, on September 17th, the rock group The Doors courted controversy by appearing on the Ed Sullivan show with frontman Jim Morrison singing a drug-related lyric in defiance of the host's wishes; that same night The Who destroyed their instruments while performing on The Smothers Brothers Comedy Hour, climaxing in an unexpectedly jarring explosion of Keith Moon's drum kit; while several months earlier, a relative unknown named Jimi Hendrix shocked audience members at the Monterey Pop Festival in California by dry-humping his amplifier and setting fire to his prized guitar. Wild things, indeed.

Seen in this context, the first major film appearance of an alleged Bigfoot now seems like an apt symbol for the entire period. Midway between human and animal, this creature mirrored a powerful instinctual energy surging forth in the collective psyche, yet one coupled with a newly awakened sense of individuality and independent thought. Remember, this wasn't simply a beast, but an apparently intelligent one that walked upright like ourselves. Similarly, people of that time were trying to juggle starkly polarized energies in themselves, born from that divide between our loftiest creative impulses and our most primal passions.

Astrologically, the Patterson-Gimlin encounter took place during a powerful astrological alignment between the planets Uranus and Pluto—a celestial duo typically associated with revolutionary change and volatile emotions, such as occurred in France during the 1790's. As I write this essay now (2013), the world finds itself in the midst of the next major configuration involving these planets to occur since the 1960's, as they reconnect now in a 90-degree angle. Not surprisingly, we not only see signs of civil unrest in countries around the world but, curiously enough, the phenomenon of Bigfoot has reached an all-time high, with TV series, books, and pop culture references to the creature popping up seemingly everywhere.

The Loch Ness Monster

The Patterson-Gimlin incident provides a useful springboard for considering another mainstay of Fortean lore: Scotland's legendary Loch Ness Monster. While sightings of the creature actually date back centuries, modern fascination with this phenomenon began in 1933—specifically May 2nd, when journalist Alex Campbell first applied the term "monster" in an article he wrote for the *Inverness Courier*.

As it turned out, 1933 was a pivotal year in a number of key respects. Less than six weeks before Campbell's article was published, Adolph Hitler began his establishment as dictator of Germany, on March 23rd, with the passing of the Enabling Act. And just three weeks before that, on March 2nd, the world was introduced to a Fortean creature of a strictly fictional sort, with the film premiere of *King Kong*.

With that in mind, the "coming out" of the Loch Ness creature in 1933 offers a surreal metaphor for the spirit of that era. Like the mid-1960's, this was a time of powerful emotional energies rising to the surface, in both constructive and destructive ways. The advent of Hitler and the premiere of *King Kong* during the exact same month synchronistically parallel one another, I'd suggest, since both represented figures of immense power that grew out of control and terrorized civilized society, but which then ultimately destroyed themselves. In the midst of this, the Scottish leviathan surfacing into public consciousness can be seen as a portent for the turbulent times that loomed ahead.

It hardly seems coincidental that 1933 was also accompanied by a tight configuration between those same powerhouse planets, Uranus and Pluto, similar to what occurred when that other oversized primate made its screen debut for Roger Patterson and Bob Gimlin in 1967. What goes around comes around.

One Step Beyond

I've suggested here at least two different levels of importance to Fortean events—the personal and the collective. But I'd like to touch briefly on another possible level of significance: the *universal*. What does that mean? Simply, that Fortean events of the most dramatic kind may be saying something important—perhaps even revolutionary—about the nature of the cosmos itself. Let me explain.

In some instances, an unusual event may simply be that: an unusual event, something out of the ordinary but nothing fundamentally radical. For thousands of years people saw rocks falling from the sky, and these reports were dismissed as nonsensical even by such distinguished thinkers as Thomas Jefferson. Yet scientists eventually discovered those falling rocks were actually quite natural, and labeled them "meteorites." There wasn't anything paranormal or truly mysterious about them, so much as unknown. Likewise, reports of the mountain gorilla were considered anecdotal and anomalous until proof for their existence finally came to light in 1902 (during yet another configuration involving Uranus and Pluto, wouldn't you know). As a result, phenomena which at one time may have been considered paranormal or "Fortean" aren't any longer.

But then there are Fortean events of a very different order, phenomena of such inherent mystery and high strangeness that they fly in the face of all science and logic. In this category we might include stories of "time slips" where events or individuals from other eras intersect with our own; rainfalls of frogs or fish from the sky; sightings of angelic beings; or bizarre animals so fantastic they stretch credulity to the breaking point.

One example of this last category would be stories of Mothman, a large humanoid creature with glowing red eyes and wings reportedly sighted in West Virginia during the 1960's and that's been glimpsed since then in other regions as well. The fact that a man-size creature with wings could even become airborne seems patently absurd on its surface, yet scores of witnesses swear to what they saw and their stories coincide in intriguing ways. (It's worth noting that the bulk of these sightings preceded a major tragedy in December of 1967, when the Silver Bridge collapsed into West Virginia's Ohio River, killing 46 people—leading some to speculate whether the creature's appearance may have been an omen for the impending disaster.)

While I can't speak to the objective truth of bizarre sightings like this, I confess that I'm not as inclined to dismiss them out of hand as some are, after having had an encounter with a mystery animal once myself and which remains unexplained to me even today.

I was 29 years old at the time, and visiting a former teacher of mine from Chicago, Maureen Cleary, at her new home in Colorado where she lived with her two young girls. The four of us decided to take a drive up through the nearby mountains one afternoon, following a narrow road that carried us progressively higher, when at one point we all noticed a large black dog cross from one side of the road to the other, roughly 70 feet in front of our car. Nothing really unusual about that (other than the presence of a dog in such a remote location). But on reaching the other side of the road, the dog simply disappeared into the side of the mountain. Maura, myself, and her children all looked at one another in puzzlement, because it seemed as if the dog had vanished into thin air—or into solid rock, as the case may be.

There was no real vegetation or brush in that spot, so my first sense was it must have crawled into some hidden crevasse or gully that we simply couldn't see from our vantage point. But as we slowly drove past where the animal disappeared, it became obvious there was no place it could have gone to, since there was no crevasse or gully there, just solid rock. Just to make sure, though, we stopped the car and got out to look around, but that only deepened the mystery. I knew what I had seen, and Maura was an intelligent observer herself, having taught psychology during her academic days. And her two children saw the dog, too, making four witnesses to the event in all.

What was it? I still don't have any good explanation for it. On a personal level, I detect a certain symbolic meaningfulness in it, since it happened at a turning point in my life when I was undergoing major emotional changes and self-reflection with my 30th birthday fast approaching (as I'll talk about in a later chapter). As one possibility, the image of "crossing the road" could be interpreted as a transitional symbol, similar to the crossing of a river or a country's borders. In fact, just one week earlier I'd hiked into the Grand Canyon and experienced a personal epiphany of sorts while crossing a footbridge suspended over the Colorado River at Canyon's bottom. Historically, too, there is a considerable body of folklore involving apparitions or sightings of large black dogs. There are several possible ways of interpreting the event.

But apart from its possible meaning for us as individuals, I've often wondered a great deal about what an event like this means in terms of *reality itself.* Perhaps what Fortean phenomena of high strangeness like this tell us is that we don't know nearly as much about the universe as we thought. Our conventional world may overlap with other dimensions and vibrational realms similar to the way radio and television waves surround us now, though we may be unaware of them.

Fortean events could represent tears in the fabric of reality which allow other dimensions to bleed through into ours, reflecting a true cross-pollination of dimensions. Such experiences seem to occur during times that feel special or filled with numinosity, or what the Greeks described as *kairos*, sacred time. They seem to possess an archetypal resonance, allowing us to expand the boundaries of our consciousness and catch momentary glimpses of the larger ocean of possibilities we swim within. In the end, Fortean events may represent portals into a different way of understanding our universe, and ultimately, ourselves.

This essay first appeared in the anthology Darklore, Volume 8, *editor: Greg Taylor, Daily Grail Publishing, 2014.*

CHAPTER 6

A GLIMPSE OF GNOSIS

Gnosis (noun) def. - deeper wisdom; a direct knowledge of spiritual truth

I've sometimes heard it said that the most important insights tend to happen when you least expect them, and that's certainly been true for me. Like the time I was walking down a street in my local neighborhood after having just read a book on mysticism and Eastern philosophy, which set me thinking about the question of God. Now, I had strongly believed in the *possibility* of God for some time by that point, since my background in the arts suggested there was just too much beauty and design in the world for there *not* to be some extraordinary intelligence underlying it all. Even if there wasn't actually a "God," then there must surely be something *God-like* behind all these extraordinary wonders and patterns around me, from the dance of the stars and planets in the sky to the grandeur of the Grand Canyon, to the jaw-dropping coincidences weaving continually throughout my life.

Following that line of thinking, a chain of insights began unfolding for me. I thought: if God exists, then by definition there can't be anything *outside* of God. That is, if he/she is truly all-encompassing and all-pervading, then by definition *everything* must be an expression of "God."

As that idea began sinking in, everything around me slowly seemed to look brighter, clearer, as though it was infused with an inner luminosity. That was because, I realized, God must be *everywhere*—in the buildings around me, the sky and clouds above me, even in those cars rushing past me.

74

But this led to another shift, namely: if it's all God, then *I, too,* must be God. Not in some exclusive, megalomaniacal way, but in the sense that everything in existence must be God, an expression of that Divine ground—and that included me. In short, *I am God. But so are you, and so is every other being!*

This was like a quiet bomb going off in my head. From stories like those I'd just finished reading, I knew this wasn't full-blown enlightenment, let alone "cosmic consciousness," but it was full-blown enough to pry my mind open to a different way of thinking about the Divine. Up to then—in no small part because of that parochial upbringing—I'd always regarded God as something outside myself, different in some fundamental way from me. But now I realized that the reality I'm experiencing right now—*this very being, this very consciousness*—is an expression of "God," of life, of *reality.* There was even something humorous about all of this, because it suggested that what I'd been searching for all along was the very thing doing the looking.

So what had begun simply as a conceptual exercise eventually shifted into something more visceral and experiential—and with that came an almost intoxicating sense of empowerment. Why "empowerment"? Because I knew that if I am indeed God, or Reality, then I am privy to all the powers, potentials, and knowledge of God—and that's true for everyone else as well. In a way, nothing really seemed impossible to me anymore. I almost felt compelled to run up to people on the street and shake them by the shoulders and say, "Hey, wake up! *You are God!*"

Afterwards I felt it was almost impossible to explain that experience to others, since there was something so inherently paradoxical about it. After all, how could everyone be God, the ultimate Center? Years later I stumbled across a mythological image from the East that conveyed that paradox well. Hinduism speaks of Indra's "Net of Jewels," which is said to be infinite in every direction and where every jewel at every nodal point reflects the entire net. That image expresses that quality of both wholeness and individuality at the same time, and resonated closely with my experience that day. Each of us is a jewel in that net, and each of us contains the whole in some profound way. On arriving home later that first day, though, I wrote in my diary: "The entire cosmos is looking through my eyes right now, and looking through your eyes right now."

It was around then I recalled something Shelly Trimmer said to me, which made no sense at the time but which now was clear. He cited an ancient teaching of mystic geometry that suggested "God can be symbolized by a circle whose center is everywhere but whose circumference is nowhere." That resonated with my own experience, since I also had the sense that *every point in existence* was the center of all existence. Said another way, there is nowhere that "God" *isn't*.

During a conversation I had with Goswami Kriyananda shortly after, I decided to ask him about my experience. He reiterated that, yes, it was legitimate, but it was a tiny glimpse. Many people have the "seed insight" that they are God, or Reality, but it's another thing to realize what that means in a fuller sense, he explained. There's a difference between a drop of water and the larger ocean it came from. But experiencing that single drop can be valuable, since it opens the door to that larger awakening.

Alas, that larger awakening never really happened, not to the degree I hoped, anyway. The vividness of that initial experience faded in intensity for me over the coming weeks and months. But I never completely lost touch with its essential message—namely, that the Truth always lies close to home.

Very close.

This essay first appeared in Quest magazine, Winter 2018.

CHAPTER 7

THE MYTHOLOGIST

"A myth is somebody else's religion."

The man on the car radio uttering that remark did so with a certain wry charm that caught my attention, not just for its wit but for its genuine insight. He tossed it off in the most offhand of ways, yet it made a valid point about how blind we often are to our own belief systems. So who was this fellow?

It was nearly two years before I learned the voice on the radio belonged to Joseph Campbell, a scholar of mythology at Sarah Lawrence College. I'd perused a few books and articles on mythology up till that point, and I was always intrigued by how mythological themes seemed to crop up in movies. Like the time I heard film director Robert Wise deliver a lecture on the city's north side and describe his surprise on hearing someone point out the parallels between his film *The Day the Earth Stood Still* and the life story of Jesus, which they hadn't thought of at all while making the movie. Despite that, mythology was never quite the burning passion for me that it was for some of my peers, who insisted it was one of those subjects that all serious thinkers should be deeply versed in. As embarrassed as I was to admit it, those stories about long-forgotten gods and goddesses just left me cold.

That is, until I encountered Joseph Campbell. After reading just the first few pages of volume one of his *Masks of God* series, I was hooked. Writers like Mircea Eliade, Frithjof Schuon, and Claude Lévi-Stauss conveyed their ideas in a more academic fashion, but Campbell's insights and reader-friendly style ignited a fire in me for the meaning and symbolism of those tales like nothing else had. He spoke with such an infectious sense of wonderment that it felt like setting foot onto an exotic new continent with each new cultural mythology he mapped out.

Before long, I was driven to get my hands on everything he'd written. Up until then, my thinking had been profoundly impacted by figures like Goswami Kriyananda and Shelly Trimmer, not to mention college teachers like Stan Brakhage, John Luther-Scofill, and Maureen Cleary. Joseph Campbell was turning out to be the next one in line to crack open my thinking in a powerful way.

The Campbell Seminars
During the late 1970s and early 1980s I jumped at every chance to study with whatever teachers happened to be passing through town, which included such figures as John Lilly, Gary Zukav, Ram Dass, Namkai Norbu, Robert Anton Wilson, Jean Houston, Michael Harner, James Hillman, and Dane Rudhyar, among others. But it was in 1981 that I learned that Campbell came into Chicago every year to present lectures and seminars on the city's north side. Naturally, I was quick to sign up.

The routine was much the same each time. He'd deliver a public lecture on a Friday night, followed by a seminar in greater depth on the same topic for the rest of the weekend. Since he was still relatively unknown in the Chicagoland area, the attendance at those weekend seminars was usually modest, with anywhere from twenty to thirty people crowded together in a room on the Loyola University campus just off of Chicago's lakefront. One year he'd discuss the work of James Joyce, the next year the psychology of the chakras, and another time the Arthurian legends, and so on.

His vitality and enthusiasm were remarkable, as was his ability to rattle off volumes of information on a wide range of topics without relying on notes. Trying to keep up with him felt at times like trying to drink from a firehose. Even his passing asides were provocative, intellectual depth charges that released their power only on later reflection—like his offhand remark that "Hitler set out to create the Third Reich but gave birth to the state of Israel instead"; or, "myth is the opening through which the transcendent truths of the universe pour into manifestation." Of course, *follow your bliss* was the one that eventually became a household meme, but wound up being repeated so often over the ensuing years that it began to sound a bit more like fingernails on a chalkboard than the inspirational trope he intended.

Then there were the anecdotes, a seemingly bottomless well of them. During one workshop he made passing reference to the fact that singer Bob Dylan "saved the Bollingen Foundation from going out of business." The Bollingen Foundation was a publishing house and educational organization devoted to the works of Carl Jung. Campbell left the comment dangling for a few seconds before finally explaining that Bollingen had been on the brink of bankruptcy a couple of decades earlier, when Dylan unexpectedly remarked during an interview with *Rolling Stone* magazine how much he liked the *I Ching*—the traditional Chinese book of divination and wisdom. At that time, the most conspicuous translation of it on the shelves was by Richard Wilhelm and Cary Baynes, published by Bollingen. Dylan's passing comment was enough to catapult sales of the book, so that after teetering on the brink of bankruptcy, Bollingen suddenly found itself awash in money. That's show biz.

But I began to see I'd never quite see eye-to-eye with Campbell on *everything.* He clearly had no love for popular culture and seemed to reserve a special distaste for the countercultural '60s—the hippie movement in particular. More worrisome was the hard right-wing sensibility I sometimes sensed beneath the surface of some passing comments. That was confirmed for me years later when I learned how he sent a letter of congratulations to President Nixon upon the bombing of Cambodia. Yowzer. Shocking as revelations like that were, though, it didn't diminish my respect for his teachings on mythology, since those were cut from a very different cloth.

The Critique

Because of the small size of the groups, it was not only possible to ask questions during his talks but relatively easy to corner him during a break to speak with him in private. On one occasion I worked up the nerve to seek out his feedback on a short piece I'd written just a few nights earlier, concerning Stanley Kubrick's film *2001: A Space Odyssey.* Since first seeing it as a teenager, when I was lucky enough to win tickets for the Chicago premiere, I read everything I could about the film and was fascinated by the story's symbolism and how it touched on classic mystic themes. With those thoughts swirling in my head, I sat down and wrote a few paragraphs detailing my ideas about the film and how it symbolized the hero's journey to enlightenment. It went like this:

> *The film's central character, the astronaut Bowman, is shown journeying to the planet Jupiter—in traditional astrology, the planet most commonly associated with God. (In Sanskrit, fittingly, the word for Jupiter is "Guru.") But before he can complete this epic journey, Bowman must first slay the modern equivalent of the traditional 'dragon'—a high-tech computer named HAL. Unlike the dragon of traditional myths, more of a symbol for primal emotions and instincts, the computer represents a more modern challenge: the hyper-rational mind. Bowman's act of disengaging HAL speaks to the need to 'unplug' the mind before one can reach Jujpiter, or enlightenment.*
>
> *Once that's achieved, Bowman is able to enter the mysterious stargate—symbolizing transcendence itself. Once there, he undergoes a transformation and is reborn as a star child. At film's end, he returns to Earth as an alien-like embryo, and is shown floating high above the earth—apparently a "Bodhisatwa" now returning to help the world. The mystic arc is complete, the hero now having been transformed by his quest.*

(There's even a hint of archetypal sexuality in all of this, I added, since the large spaceship housing Bowman for most of his journey is phallic-shaped, and on arriving at his destination the astronaut is ejected like a sperm cell and plunged into the vagina-like "stargate"—depicted initially as two vertical walls—after which a cosmic infant pops out, the aforementioned starchild. Both Freud *and* Jung would have had a field day with that, no doubt.)

I felt quite proud of my little commentary, and couldn't wait to get Campbell's feedback about it, never for a moment thinking how presumptuous it might be to think he'd find it all that original. So during a break one afternoon, I handed him a copy, which he politely accepted. The next day during a break while standing near him, I secretly hoped he would volunteer some feedback. When that didn't happen, I edged closer, then nervously mustered up the nerve to ask if he had a chance to look over my short piece.

"Excuse me, but did you have a chance to read my paper?"

"Oh, yes—I read it last night!"

He was upbeat, but there was no sign of a verdict one way or the other. That was concerning. I decided to go for broke and ask him outright what he thought. Obviously trying to be diplomatic, he paused and said, "Well, you know...they *based the movie on my work.*"

What could I say to something like that? I might have been embarrassed or dejected, but he was so gracious that I simply said, "Oh!" Not only was my theory about the film nothing new to him, but the movie was inspired by his own research. (Well, maybe, maybe not. A colleague I later mentioned this exchange to questioned whether world-class geniuses like Stanley Kubrick and Arthur C. Clarke really needed an outside thinker to come up with an archetypal story like theirs. After all, Campbell didn't *invent* the hero's journey, he simply chronicled it. That made me wonder whether Campbell's suspicions about his work and that film might have been a bit like the motorist who buys a red Volkswagen and starts noticing every other red Volkswagen on the road. Perhaps the hero's quest had been such a prominent fixture in his own mind that when he saw it cropping up in a major Hollywood film, he assumed it was influenced by his own writings on the subject—whether that was true or not. The irony is that Campbell himself taught that similar themes appear in places far removed from one another in time and space, and don't necessarily require a causal connection. Did that happen here? We'll probably never know for sure.)

The Apparent Intentionality of Fate

Of all the ideas Campbell discussed in those talks, the one that left the greatest impact on me stemmed from a passing remark he made about the German philosopher Arthur Schopenhauer, and an essay he wrote titled "Transcendental Speculation on the Apparent Intentionality in the Fate of the Individual." Schopenhauer suggested that when seen through the lens of hindsight, one's life can take on the appearance of a carefully constructed novel, as though the seemingly unintended events and accidents of one's early life were really integral elements of a larger unfolding destiny. Campbell went on to quote the philosopher:

"Would it not be an act of narrow-minded cowardice to maintain it would be impossible for the life paths of all mankind in their complex interrelationships to exhibit as much concert and harmony as a composer can bring into the any apparently disconnected and haphazardly turbulent voices of his symphony?"

Who was this "composer," I wondered? I found myself coming back to Schopenhauer's passage repeatedly over the years, and would eventually incorporate it into my own writings about synchronicity and destiny, where it would play a key role.

He mentioned those ideas of Schopenhauer's during a weekend where we explored the parallels between James Joyce's *Ulysses* and Homer's *Odyssey*. In addition to explaining how the symbolic stages in each of these works mirrored one another, Campbell also hinted at the richly interlocking worldview that Joyce portrayed in *Ulysses*. That perspective resonated beautifully with ideas I'd been developing around the subject of synchronicity for the book I'd begun working on, *The Waking Dream*. I was especially fascinated by Joyce's way of interweaving disparate events as if orchestrated by some great cosmic novelist. I felt certain that it must reveal something important about Joyce's own view of life as well, so when I finally had the chance to question Campbell about that privately, I asked whether he believed Joyce's two books *Ulysses* and *Finnegans Wake* truly reflected a symbolist and synchronistic vision of life. He nodded cautiously, but was careful to clarify:

"Well, yes, that's certainly true of *Ulysses*, but it's not really true of *Finnegans Wake*."

How's that?

"*Ulysses* deals with the mythic aspect of our 'day' world, of waking life. But *Finnegans Wake* plunges you down fully to the world of dreams, completely into that deep mythic realm."

After spending some more time with both of those difficult books, I eventually understood what Campbell meant. In *Ulysses*, the reader at least has some reference points to ordinary reality, but in *Finnegans Wake* the reader is cut loose almost entirely from worldly moorings and set adrift in the deep waters of the collective unconscious. *Finnegans Wake* is not so much a statement about our everyday world as about the cosmic ocean underlying it. (Sadly, while reading those books again helped me understand that synchronistic connection better, it didn't do much to improve my opinion of the books themselves, at least not *Finnegans Wake*. Why? Because for all of the extraordinary scholarship they displayed, when a work becomes so obtuse that only a handful of elite scholars around the world can decipher its far-flung meanings, I have to wonder whether it's crossed the line from "art" to a cryptographic puzzle intended for a very, very few.)

The Power of Myth

Campbell's energy was such that when he died of cancer in 1986, it came as a surprise. As it so happened, it was finally in death that he attained the worldwide fame he seemed destined for, thanks to Bill Moyers' series of TV interviews called *The Power of Myth* in 1988. Among other things, it was that show which first informed viewers that filmmaker George Lucas drew inspiration for *Star Wars* partly from Campbell's work. And in contrast with Kubrick and Clarke's script for *2001*, George Lucas openly admitted to that influence, so there was no disputing matters this time around.

Aside from the unexpected news of his death, I was also surprised by some of the criticism I saw being directed at Campbell from various quarters, some of which concerned his personal opinions on politics and race (such as from Brendan Gill in *The New Yorker*), but much of it even aimed at his scholarly approach towards myth and religion. A leading voice in that debate was Wendy Doniger, who was a world-famous scholar on mythology and religion, and who was considered by many to be his chief "rival" in mythological circles. I interviewed her in 1990 for the Theosophical publication *The Quest*, and when I brought up Campbell, she was mildly respectful but criticized his "universalist" approach towards myth and religion, which she described as being more concerned with the similarities between mythologies rather than their differences. Being more of a "particularist" herself, she felt the differences between myths were where the *real* action is, not the similarities, and even seemed to imply Campbell never even bothered to study the nuances and distinctions between cultural mythologies. [1]

Problem is, that's not accurate. While Campbell did lean more towards the "universalist" approach, he was well aware of the differences between mythologies and often cited Adolf Bastian's distinction between "elementary ideas" and "folk ideas"—the former referring to the universal patterns in myths and the latter referring to the local variations on those universal themes. A good example of Campbell's keen eye in this regard was his discussion of the Knights of the Round Table from the Arthurian legends. He noted that the Knights rode out in search of the Grail as individuals rather than as a group, and contrasted that with heroic sagas of the past like Jason and his band of Argonauts searching for the Golden Fleece, where the heroes sailed out as a group. To Campbell, that contrast between older and newer heroic quests reflected a dramatic shift in consciousness, and a movement towards greater individualism in Western culture.

In some cases, I had to wonder about the real motives behind those criticisms, and even wondered whether they might have been based more on professional jealousy than scholarship. I once spoke with a philosophy professor who confided to me that "few things will annoy your colleagues in academia more than becoming really popular and successful." Needless to say, Joseph Campbell became really popular and successful.

Though I didn't continue following this subject as obsessively as I did back then, my way of thinking continued to draw on mythic and archetypal currents in a variety of ways. That's been especially true for me while looking at cultural trends and understanding how modern stories sometimes echo ancient themes. I'd find myself looking at Walt Disney's animated film *The Lion King* and notice how closely it resonated with the Egyptian tales of Osiris, as well as Shakespeare's *Hamlet,* with its story of a son avenging an evil uncle who murdered his father; or I'd be watching Wim Wenders's film *Paris, Texas* and notice how closely it resembled the ancient tale of Odysseus, and a man struggling to find his way home in a semi-amnesiac state, then meeting up with the woman he loved while hiding his identity.

But I've also been fascinated by how our collective mythologies seem to be *changing* in subtle ways, where we see shifts in the inflection of archetypal themes over time rather than simple reiterations. Campbell's example of the Knights of the Round Table from centuries ago was one example of that, but that transformation has been continuing into present times. For instance, religion has itself been undergoing significant changes, with a clear shift towards a more democratic and kaleidoscopic approach towards faith and worship. Even our conception of God has been transforming, to the point where it's not unusual now for a religious figure or pop celebrity to publicly state that "God lies within"—quite a contrast to publicly expressed views on God four or five centuries ago, when such notions might have gotten one burned at the stake. Changes like these point to tectonic shifts deep beneath the surface of popular consciousness—a point I explore more fully in my book *Signs of the Times*.

It's all left me wrestling with a question that occurred to me decades ago, but which I still ponder: to what degree do our mythologies liberate us, and to what degree do they limit or imprison us?

I'd love to have gotten Joseph Campbell's answer to that one.

This essay first appeared in Quest magazine, Summer 2018.

CHAPTER 8

SOUTHWESTERN ODYSSEY
A SIGHTSEER'S JOURNEY INTO
THE UNDERWORLD

When my 30th birthday approached, I began to feel as though I was on the verge of imploding. My first and only relationship of five years was falling apart, and I watched from the sidelines as other people my age were moving up the professional ladder while I struggled mightily to gain a foothold on any rung at all. Amplifying that anxiety was the heart attack my father suffered that year. Although he survived, it faced me with my own mortality like nothing else before.

As a result, I felt desperate to make a change, genuinely believing this was a life-or-death matter to resolve. I took what money I had saved up and decided to spend it on something I'd been contemplating for a while: travel. I hoped desperately that a change of scenery might help clear my head and open me up to new possibilities, and perhaps even help provide fuel for the writing projects I'd begun fantasizing about.

I embarked on two trips that year, the first of those in the Spring which took me through the American Southwest for six weeks, and the second one later that same year which was a three-month backpacking trip around the world that took me through England, India, Nepal, China, the Philippines, Japan and Hawaii. Both trips had a dramatic impact on me, but the first one, although shorter, was even more powerful in a number of ways, oddly enough. What follows is a description of that trip, which began on April 1st of 1982 and ran through to the end of May.

⇒╬╬⇐

The morning I was set to leave, I dreamt that I was having sex with a powerful black woman, with blazing tongues of fire on her head in place of hair. I could feel the heat, yet I was never burned. It almost felt like an initiation, and was both ecstatic and terrifying at once. I awakened with a jolt, and the lingering feelings were so pungent that I sat on the edge of my bed for several minutes wondering what it meant, and whether it foreshadowed anything about the weeks directly ahead of me.

The Sun was setting low on the horizon as I drove out onto the interstate, heading out from the Chicago suburbs towards the American Southwest. Late winter flurries swirled across the road as I pulled away from the city and out onto the open plains. As night fell, the sky cleared and through my windshield I could see Jupiter sparkling next to the Moon. I drove straight on through the night.

On reaching Colorado the next day, I turned left at the Rockies and headed south towards New Mexico. The scenery soon changed dramatically with the lush greens up north making way for the sandy ochres of the desert. This was a different world altogether, with its own distinctive vegetative, wildlife, and color palette, with vast horizons stretching in all directions. After the comparatively bland Midwest, this landscape truly does feel enchanted, just like the license plates there proclaim.

Over the previous year, I had begun work on my first book, *The Waking Dream*, which would explore the role of synchronicities and symbols in our lives. In planning out this trip, I started to see it as a possible "synchronistic laboratory" where I could actually test out some of the theories and observations I was developing, since trips (and pilgrimages) seemed to be especially fertile breeding ground for synchronistic events and numinous experiences of many types. In fact, my life that previous year had almost begun feeling like a science project of sorts, but of a more esoteric sort, devoted toward the study of patterns of experience and consciousness rather than just physical phenomena. As I drove deeper into New Mexico, I increasingly sensed those next few weeks could become an especially rich opportunity in this way, even if I had no idea how that might actually play out.

Relics of Bygone Cultures

At one point I noticed the ruins of an old school house several hundred yards off the side of the road. There was something vaguely eerie about the scene, with the abandoned structure situated out in the middle of nowhere against a crystal blue sky, with white clouds high in the distance. I parked my car and walked over with my camera to take a closer look.

Making my way towards it, I snapped a few pictures, when I was jolted by the sound of a vast "boom" roaring out of the sky so loud it caused the ground to rumble. It sounded like multiple thunderclaps firing all at once, and echoed across the landscape for at least 15 seconds. I had never heard anything that loud; I fully expected to look up and see a mushroom cloud rising over the horizon, perhaps the result of an atomic experiment gone awry. This was New Mexico, after all.

Yet the sky remained clear, with no sign of an explosion anywhere. I'd heard sonic booms many times before, and even knew what dynamiting at construction sites sounded like, but this was different. I had no idea what the source might be, and it left me with an unsettled feeling for hours afterwards.

I continued on my journey and over the next few days spent time exploring some of the Native American ruins around the region—Puye, Bandelier, Betatakin, Chaco Canyon, the "sky city" Acoma, and Canyon de Chelly. I'd always been fascinated by these locations whenever I read about them, but never had the opportunity to investigate them up close before. Most had been abandoned for centuries before being restored by archeologists over the last century, and all of them are permeated with the ambience of lingering human dramas.

Bandelier National Monument, New Mexico

I learned early on that the best way to experience sites like these is to arrive early, before other tourists showed up. That way one can experience them with fewer distractions or chattering bystanders. As a result, I was able to spend hours at these sites exploring them largely by myself, accompanied only by the sounds of blowing wind and circling hawks. The elemental feel of this region is unique; one almost senses a subtle electricity crackling in the atmosphere. It's not hard to imagine that spirits still inhabit these lands; in my mind's eye it seemed as though everything was outlined by a subtle glow.

There are times when we crave certain geographies much like our body craves specific foods or minerals; perhaps it's the soul's way of restoring psychic equilibrium. After the manicured perfections of the big city and its suburbs, I felt drawn to the vast antiquity and deep places of this land, including the subterranean temples called *kivas* where the ancient peoples conducted their religious ceremonies. It's fascinating how the sacred spots of Christianity like the great cathedrals of Europe ascend high into the sky while those of the Native Americans extend down into the Earth. I've even wondered whether there might be some geomantic significance to the fact that this region harbors that mother of all deep places—the Grand Canyon. Could that extraordinary feature shape the imaginations and psyches of everyone who's lived in this region, in the same way that the soaring peaks of the Himalayas seem to shape the spirits of those living there? I was hoping to find some answers to that question myself, when I descended into the Grand Canyon myself, which was still a week or two away.

The Sufi House

Before leaving on my trip I had read a number of books on Sufism, the mystical branch of Islam. Although it has a more devotional aspect, Sufism doesn't ignore the rational mind, and that appealed to me. While doing a little research, I learned that a community of young Sufis lived in the desert just south of Sante Fe, so I made arrangements by phone and mail several weeks earlier to stay with them for a few days.

Turning off the main two-lane blacktop south of the city onto a dirt road, I came upon a sprawling ranch home presided over by four young women with exotic names like Nanda, Kismet, Shimat, and Habiba, though it turned out their given names were Nancy, Rebecca, Janet, and Michelle. They seemed happy to have a man on the premises. Outside of their house I noticed a few small huts and tents spread out in the adjoining desert, and Habiba explained they were occupied by men and women on extended private retreats. Every day it was part of her devotional work to bring them food or supplies.

As for me, I'd be staying in the big house with the women, she said, and she showed me the small room I'd be using for the next few days. Stepping into the room, I was immediately taken aback by a distinct spiritual energy, as if a tangible force field hit me square and center. It reminded me of an experience I had one year earlier, walking into the Cathedral of St. John the Divine in New York City, where I felt a similarly palpable sense of the sacred. This time was more surprising, though, since it happened in such a modest and unassuming space—a plain room barely larger than a closet. When I mentioned my experience to Habiba, she said, "Hmm…The last guy who stayed in that room used to meditate for up to six hours a day in there."

Over the next few days I tried meditating in that room myself, but my mind was so restless that I simply wound up feeling frustrated. Instead, I wound up spending most of my time listening to cassette recordings of talks from the in-house library by a prominent Sufi teacher, Pir Vilayat Khan, who I'd met several years earlier in Chicago when he came to town for a lecture. His recorded talks focused primarily on working with inner energies, employing mantras and visualizations. One of the techniques was similar to one I'd learned in the Kriya Yoga tradition, involving moving energies up and down the spine. A few days later I would try this technique in a large ceremonial kiva at Chaco Canyon, and felt a noticeable surge of energy throughout my body, almost as if I were absorbing energy from the Earth itself. I normally hadn't felt any-thing quite so tangible with techniques like that before, but in that spot I did. What made the difference, I wondered—the location or the technique? Maybe both.

The night before I was set to leave the house, the young women told me about two Hopi elders from Arizona who were scheduled to speak in Santa Fe that coming weekend, where they were to discuss the so-called "Hopi Prophecy." I wanted to stay and hear them, hopefully even speak with them, since it might help fuel the research and writing I was doing. While planning this trip, I'd dreamt of meeting with figures in the Native American and Tibetan communities in hope of learning more about their per-spectives towards omens, oracles, and divination. But my hunch this time was to move on, so the next day I left the Sufi house and headed out west from Sante Fe, stopping off for a couple of days to visit the town of Taos, high up in the hills.

Taos Pueblo, Taos, New Mexico

Three Little Stones

An odd thing happened over the course of those next few days. While in the restored ruins of the Great Kiva in Chaco Canyon, I decided to pick up three small stones from the center of the site, and take them home with me as treasured mementos of my experience there. At first, I wondered whether that was appropriate, since I'd heard stories about bad luck befalling those who took items from sacred sites, such as pieces of pottery or bits of brick from an ancient dwelling, not to mention truly sacred objects. But these were simply small stones in the dirt, not artifacts, I said to myself, so I pushed those concerns out of my mind.

Several days later while visiting Canyon de Chelly in Arizona, I parked my car in one of the designated areas for tourists and hiked down into the Canyon, taking in both the ancient ruins and the extraordinary natural vistas. When I returned to my car several hours later, I was startled to discover one of the side windows of my car had been shattered and some valuables of mine inside were stolen—exactly three, in fact: my binoculars, a cassette recorder, and a case holding an expensive camera lens. As disappointing as this was, it was hard not noticing that I lost the same number of items I carried away from the Great Kiva at Chaco. When I returned home to Illinois several weeks later, I made a point of placing those three stones in a padded envelope and sent them back to the ranger offices at Chaco Canyon, asking that they be returned to the spot where I took them. No harm in hedging one's bets.

The Hopi Reservation

I eventually found my way to the Hopi reservation in central Arizona. I was unsure where to start when exploring this region, due to its great size, so I drove around the three primary mesas which dominate this reservation to familiarize myself with the area.

The poverty there was dramatic. The entire landscape was spare, with a few abandoned vehicles near the roads. Yet despite such features there's an undeniable mystique to the region. Some of that may be due to the sheer austerity of the desert itself, which I find deeply moving in its own way. But I sensed there was more to it than that, and wondered whether it could be the result of ancestral memories and the stored vibrations from all the rituals, visions, and beliefs that suffused this landscape for millennia?

I stopped off at the local Native American cultural center hoping they might point me in the right direction. I mentioned to the fellow behind the counter that I was a writer doing research and hoped to speak with some of the locals. That's when I discovered how wary some tribal members are towards outsiders—especially writers. Many of these residents have been exploited by journalists through the years, and that seemed to be this fellow's attitude, too. He strongly discouraged me from looking any further, and abruptly cut our conversation short, leaving the counter and walking into the back room with no further explanation. That took me by surprise, and I decided not to identify myself as a writer around those parts anymore.

As I spoke to more inhabitants of the region, I also came to realize that in terms of their religious views, the Hopis aren't the monolithic entity some New Age writers would have you believe. When non-Native commentators casually toss off comments like, "the Hopi believe this," or, "the Hopi people predict that," it's somewhat inane, akin to saying that "white people believe this," or "Europeans believe that..." For starters, I learned that the Hopi community is divided between *progressives* and *traditionals*, and these factions hold very different views on a number of matters. The latter group, the traditionals, is comprised of tribal members whose attitudes are similar to the Amish in some ways, in their wariness towards technology and its conveniences, and they refuse to rely on electricity at all. By contrast, the progressives were more open to modernization and have adapted to non-Native ways, and have no qualms about electricity at all.

I had the distinct feeling that the information I was looking for would here be found amongst the traditionalists, so that's where I set my sights.

The most traditional of all the tribal members live on the Third Mesa, I was told, in villages like Old Oraibi and Hotevilla. On entering both places I was greeted by signs reading "No Cameras Allowed," which was a tip-off right away. To my surprise, the first person I crossed paths with was a white anthropologist named Joanne Fisher who lived in a trailer on the outskirts of the village and had been studying the tribe for several years. When I asked her what she thought of writers like Frank Waters and Peter Matthiessen, she wasn't complimentary, saying they both "missed the boat," yet didn't elaborate how exactly. She told me I should walk over and talk with Thomas Banyaca, one of the self-appointed spokesmen for the tribe. I'd heard his name before, and after leaving Joanne I tracked him down at his small house a short distance away.

He answered the door, and seemed happy to speak. When I asked him about the Native American "worldview," he gently suggested they don't think of it quite that way, since it's not something they've formally codified. That made me realize just how naive my query was. He was preparing to leave town at that moment for a presentation he was set to deliver at a gathering out of state, so he couldn't talk long. He suggested that I seek out James Koots or Caroline Tawangyawma, two other residents in the area who were generally open to speaking with visitors from the outside.

I wasn't sure how to find either of them, so I enlisted the help of a local teenager I crossed paths with near the entrance to the village. He played loud Reggae music on the tape recorder he carried under his arm, and wasn't shy about smoking pot in front of me. But he was friendly and offered to help me find Caroline. He climbed into my car and guided me through the area, and lit up a large joint that caused a cloud of marijuana smoke to billow out from my car windows. Eventually, we pulled up to a modest desert home on the fringes of the village, and I saw a woman hunched over working in a garden next to a house.

Caroline Tawangyawma

Caroline was a rotund, gentle-looking woman in her seventies who spoke to me while tilling the soil alongside her house, a small adobe structure at desert's edge. After a while, she asked me where I was staying. When I told her that I'd camped out a fair distance away, she invited me to stay at her place instead. There's an extra bed inside, she said, and I'm welcome to use it. I felt overwhelmed by her offer, considering she didn't know me at all, and I was more than happy to accept. I wound up staying there five days altogether.

Simply to break the ice, we spoke those first few hours about a variety of subjects, and as dinnertime approached we headed inside where she lit some candles. Her home was comfortably disheveled, without a single electrical appliance anywhere. We continued talking as she began preparing a simple meal of potatoes, bread, turnips, chicken, and watermelon.

I asked her birthday, and she told me she was born on September 28th, 1906. Like many others in the tribe, she spent a considerable amount of time away from the reservation early on, living in "the white man's cities." That was another parallel with the Amish, I thought, since they also have a tradition of young people going away from the group with the option of returning. She exuded warmth, and I was deeply moved by her gentleness. Over dinner, we talked about the traditional beliefs that guided her and her neighbors. Like the others nearby, she believed that modernization had a negative effect on the spiritual life of the tribe, so they avoided it as much as possible.

"The electrical wires and telephone lines are like cobwebs that interfere with the balance of nature, with the paths of birds, and the energy here," she said. "The other villages here have appliances, housing developments, and electricity. But Hotevilla is sacred. We don't have these things."

Ironically, while uttering those words I happened to see a small pile of National Enquirers stacked on a table near the door. At first that seemed incongruous, but while speaking further with her it was obvious the residents here weren't against *all* forms of modernity, mainly electrical ones.

That night I slept on a small bed in a side room, and while lying there in the dark I heard the sounds of men in a nearby kiva singing their tribal chants, which echoed through the night.

After breakfast the next morning, I offered to drive her to the nearby tribal store and pay for her groceries. After leaving the store, I asked about her background—her family and ancestry—and she proceeded to tell me the tragic tale of how the U.S. government dealt with many of those in this village decades earlier. When we arrived back home, she pulled out a textbook on Hopi history published by the University of Arizona featuring photographs of prisoners at Alcatraz. At first I was unsure why she was showing me this, when she pointed to one ragged-looking fellow in the photo.

"That's him. That's my father."

She explained how her dad was forcibly extricated from the tribe when she was just a child, and then incarcerated at the infamous prison alongside murderers, thieves, and rapists. Why? Because he refused to allow his children to be taken away and schooled in the white man's ways, shorn of their native customs, hair, and clothing. She was surprisingly casual while describing all of this, yet I could only imagine the trauma this must have caused her family at the time.

Later that day, I happened to mention how back in Santa Fe I heard that two Hopi elders were scheduled to speak at a peace rally there that previous weekend. Did she happen to know who those two elders were, I wondered? "Well, yes. That was me and David. David Monongya. We came to town to speak about the Hopi Prophecy." Apparently my hunch about leaving Santa

Fe turned out to be good. I was eager to learn more about this so-called "Hopi Prophecy," which centers around a set of etchings carved on stone over at the Second Mesa. She asked me if I'd like to see it, and I told her yes.

The next morning we climbed into my car and she guided me to the spot where a large boulder rested, not far from Shungopavi. The imagery on this rock has become something of a Rorschach test for people over the years, with both tribal elders and outsiders offering their differing opinions about its significance and meaning. All I could make out were some stick figures and a few broken lines, but for her and fellow tribe members it was pregnant with meaning. She then told me the long story of an immense schism that developed amongst her neighbors on the reservation, catalyzed in part by this prophecy and its alleged connection to UFOs.

UFOs? I didn't see that one coming. As she explained it, a number of years earlier a few tribal members had dramatic sightings of objects in the sky, and some claimed that the prophetic markings on this large rock pointed to impending contact between UFOs and the Hopi community.

At one point during the late 1960s, a white man and his band of hippie followers entered the village, claiming to be connected somehow with the fulfillment of that prophecy. To the utter horror of the locals, the outsiders practiced their own brand of free love right out in the open. That was too much for the Hopis, both progressives and traditionals alike, and not only led to the speedy ejection of the visitors but triggered more infighting amongst the tribal members. While some remained vocal in their belief about extraterrestrials and their role in Hopi history, others were skeptical and viewed all this talk of UFOs as damaging the tribe's integrity. Whatever the truth of the matter, I thought it ironic that the most staunchly traditionalist of all the villages would also be one championing the role of hi-tech spacecraft in the Hopi's destiny.

David Monongya

I grew increasingly curious about the man she mentioned earlier, David Monongya. As she described him, he was clearly a highly respected elder in the village. He was now in his 90s and not in good health, she explained, but he's still lucid. He was living with his sister over on the other side of the village. When I asked her if it would be possible to speak with him, she said it was okay, but I should be sure to tell him that she sent me.

Following her directions, I tracked down his house the next day, and spoke with his sister at the front door. When I asked if I could see David, she initially hesitated but then agreed and escorted me into the room where the elderly David was seated. The lighting in the room reminded me of a Vermeer painting, with its diffused light and soft gray walls, with David seated there winding string off of a spool. He was nearly blind, and I knew not to stay longer than necessary. Rather than delve into any abstract questions about symbolism or divination, I decided to ask him a couple of basic questions about spirituality and every-day life.

How do you deal with disappointments, and with suffering, I asked?

"Things happen that you don't like or that make you feel bad," he replied, "but you try to offset it with a little humor, you cap it off with humor, and then you don't feel so bad. But also, you must always follow the Great Spirit, and nothing else. If you do this, things don't upset you so much, you aren't bothered by what people say, or the things that come up."

What about the deaths of loved ones? How do you view those?

"Well, when people die, they go to spiritual realm where we came from, and you don't stop loving them. When they die, you still love them, you still share your love together. That doesn't stop at death, or at least it shouldn't. And then when you die, you will go and be with them. But you're never really separated."

Like other Native Americans I've met, he spoke in simple terms, though not simplistic ones. What was slightly unsettling to me, though, was how his sister sat there looking vaguely agitated throughout this back-and-forth, and after about ten minutes I sensed it was time for me to take my leave. I shook his hand and thanked both of them for their time. As I was walking out of the room, I heard her say something in their native tongue which I couldn't understand, but the tone sounded vaguely critical. After leaving, I wondered whether I should have offered money or some gift for their time? And of course, I should have. That's the custom in most traditions, but I was too caught up in my own needs to remember that.

The Medicine Man

As enamored as I was of life in this village, I'd seen enough by this point not to romanticize it. In addition to the poverty, this community is as susceptible to interpersonal politics and backbiting as any other. That hit home for me while driving Caroline through the village one afternoon, when we passed by a certain neighbor's house. She quickly ducked down in her car seat as though trying to avoid being seen by its resident. When I asked who lived there, she spoke in guarded terms about a medicine man named Percy. He was viewed by the others in the village as a renegade since he had—horror of horrors—an electric generator on his premises. He was even suspected of being involved with magic, possibly even black magic. It's best that I just leave him alone, she cautioned.

Of course, that only made me more eager to talk with him. The next day I headed over and knocked on his door. An unassuming, soft-spoken man I guessed to be in his forties appeared, dressed in well-worn slacks and shirt. I was careful not to identify myself as a writer, and instead pulled out a small photo of my painting from back in college, "Reunion of Elements," and handed it to him as a calling card of sorts. I explained that I was an artist, and would like to have a few minutes of his time, if at all possible.

He seemed to like the artwork, stared at it a while, then walked over and placed the reproduction on his mantle. Inviting me in, I walked through the door and sat across from him over a table in his small living room. I looked around and noticed bags of medicinal herbs around the room, as well as a television set—a true oddity in this village. I began by asking about his healing work. It was fascinating to me that the first thing he said didn't involve magic or spells but rather the importance of psychology:

"It's important to determine if a patient's problem is emotional or physical in nature. If the problem is more attitudinal, then one has to work with that. Maybe the person needs to forgive others, or even themselves."

Some of his diagnostic methods seemed vaguely oriental to me, such as when he spoke about taking his fingers and trying to see which parts of a patient's body were hottest. Most striking to me, he seemed genuinely concerned with helping others; he didn't charge money for his services although he did accept bartered goods in return.

"We are only channels for the healing," he emphasized, "We're not the true healers." Those certainly didn't sound like the words of a black magician to me.

At one point, he said he had to take care of some errands outside, and asked if I'd like to walk with him over by the edge of the village. I agreed, and along the way I asked him about his view of symbolism, specifically about omens or "signs." He said, yes, they believe in those things, they come from the Divine. But there are no simple formulas for interpreting such things, he explained, one has to take them on a case-by-case basis.

Shortly after, I happened to mention a project I'd just become involved with back home and how it looked as though it could unfold very differently than I had planned. At that moment a large black bird darted past us, and suddenly changed directions in mid-air while letting out a cry. "There you go," he said, in a lively tone. "That bird changing directions just as you were talking about your project, that's telling you something. Maybe your project really will take a very different direction than you thought. That's one way of looking at it."

The next day I decided it was time for me to be on my way out of this area. Just minutes before I was set to leave, an old car pulled up in front of Caroline's home and out stepped two other tribal members—James Koots and Titus Qömayumptewa. James was thin and wiry, Titus was large and lumbered in like a large arthritic bear. The deep lines in both of their leathery faces suggested they had lived long, hard lives. Over the next hour I was deeply moved by the genuine warmth they both extended towards me. I had a wonderful conversation with them, as James spoke with pride about his years working in that "big gangster town, Chicago!" before returning to the reservation. I felt sad saying goodbye to Caroline, and as I held her hands, she shyly avoided looking me in the eyes.

The Grand Canyon

With each passing day I grew more excited about the prospect of visiting the Grand Canyon. My plan was to hike down and spend several nights camped out at the bottom. Over the years this spot had taken on near-mythic importance for me, and with my 30th birthday approaching I saw the chance to spend time down inside of it as a kind of personal vision quest.

I drove in from the far eastern end of the Canyon just as the Sun was starting to set, and the further I proceeded along the Canyon rim the more expansive and colorful the views became. By the time I reached the visitor's center, the entire Canyon was bathed in an otherworldly glow, and cloaked in deep silence.

That night I slept in the campground near the visitor's center, and had a series of intense dreams—all of them involving fire in some way, curiously. I awoke in the morning and packed my gear, then said a small prayer as I made my first steps onto the Kaibab trail that meanders down to the Canyon's bottom. As the crow flies, the distance from rim to Canyon base is a full mile, the equivalent of four Empire State Buildings stacked atop one another. The trail itself is considerably longer than that, though, since it weaves in and out much like the crow *doesn't* fly. Along the way I'd pass through three distinctly different weather systems: on top, it was snowing, midway down there was rain, and at Canyon's bottom, it was dry as a bone.

I had a growing sense over the previous weeks that something meaningful was in store for me on this leg of the trip, and that feeling only grew stronger as I drew closer towards the bottom. I decided soon after beginning my hike not to take photographs during my stay down here, since I didn't want my memories of the experience boxed in by tiny snapshots.

Making my way down step by step, I reflected on the vast spans of time indicated by the sedimentary layers visible alongside the trail. The Canyon was formed over a billion years, the books tell us, as layers of sediment were deposited by ancient oceans and the Colorado River later sliced through and exposed these rocky tissues to the open air. In a sense, this area represents a geological time machine, with each step downward taking one further back in time at the rate of thousands of years per foot. There's something paradoxical about the effect a place like this can have on one, since your ego is increasingly dwarfed by the immensity and antiquity of it all just as your soul feels enlarged by it.

Descending further, I began focusing my awareness on each step. It almost felt as though I was peeling away layers in my own psyche, with the descent symbolically plunging me deeper into some part of myself. Shedding non-essentials and going deeper—those are things I'd felt blocked about doing in my own life over the previous year, and having a ritual like this seemed to help focus my mind. Picking up a rock along the trail, I imagined that I was pouring all my negative thoughts and unpleasant memories into it, and resolved that when I crossed the footbridge at the Canyon's bottom I'd drop that rock into the river while visualizing those negative energies transformed by the river's waters.

On reaching the Canyon floor several hours later, I walked through the womb-like cave that leads to the suspension bridge spanning the two riverbanks, and stepped out over the river. Arriving in the middle of the bridge, I paused for a moment, focused my thoughts, and gently dropped the rock into the water. Looking up, I saw a flock of six white birds flying downstream towards me, which then flew under the bridge directly over the spot where I'd dropped the stone, and were then joined by a seventh bird. They continued flying downriver and disappeared around the next bend.

At the far end of the bridge, I stopped to sit and rest for a few minutes before continuing on to the nearby campground, where I found a place to pitch my tent. I struck up a conversation with a fellow in the campsite next to mine, a twenty-something with waist-length hair who'd just come off the road after following the Grateful Dead for two years. When I finally opened up to him about my experience with the Canyon, he described a realization nearly identical to mine. He'd been going through a major life-change those previous months, and himself sensed that his hike into the Canyon was somehow bringing it all to a conclusion. I was surprised when he reached into his pocket and pulled out a small rock he found while touring with the Dead, and went on to explain how he decided that upon arriving here, he would drop it into the river as a way to ritualistically signal the end of that chapter in his life.

A few minutes later we walked down to the river and he reached into his other pocket then handed me a joint, saying, "Here—you might try this at some point while you're down here. It's good stuff." Being a Deadhead, I suspected he was good for his word on that count. I put it in my pocket, and we headed back to the campsite.

I pitched my tent and noticed he was planning to sleep right out in the open, without any tent at all. When I asked him whether he was concerned about the possibility of rain, he replied, "Nah. The rangers assured me it almost never rains down here at the bottom, it evaporates before it gets this far, so I figured I'd save myself the extra load."

Shortly after midnight I heard the booming sounds of thunder, followed by a heavy downpour, along with the sound of my campsite friend scrambling to erect a makeshift shelter, muttering "*Fuck! Fuck...!*" I shouted out that he was welcome to come and stay in mine, but he declined, saying he'd manage somehow.

Trial by Fire
After breakfast I packed up my gear and began the slow ascent back up the Canyon, this time using the Bright Angel trail. It made

for a difficult climb in the growing heat, and I had to stop frequently. After a number of hours, I eventually arrived at the campground located roughly midway between the bottom and the top of the Canyon, and found a spot to pitch my tent.

Shortly before sunset I took a walk out to the promontory that extends out beyond the campground proper. I climbed up carefully onto a large boulder where I could sit and observe that part of the Canyon as the Sun set. The view before me was staggering, and within all that vastness I couldn't see a single other person anywhere. The enormous rock walls around me arched up like a cathedral, and the majestic natural forms gracing those formations seemed like the work of some cosmic Michaelangelo. It's little wonder early explorers to this region chose to identify these formations and outcrops using names like Vishnu, Brahma, and Osiris, since these forms really do evoke the qualities of gods rather than mortals. The late afternoon light cut down on a slant across this horseshoe-shaped stretch of the Canyon. Far above, I could barely make out the specter of birds gliding silently along the uppermost rim of the Canyon, which was still cloaked in snow. I've visited many beautiful natural sites in my life, but without a doubt, this was the most spectacular of them all.

I took the joint from my pocket given to me by my campsite neighbor earlier that morning and lit it up. It was more powerful than I expected, in ways both marvelous and terrifying. The late afternoon light caused the Canyon walls around me to glow as if incandescent, revealing subtle hues I hadn't noticed before. It's nearly impossible not to feel a sense of eternity in this place, I thought to myself.

But the herb was proving a bit too strong. A wave of paranoia began flooding through me, building in momentum as the minutes passed. I'd heard of anxiety attacks before—was this one of those? The tangle of worries and neurotic concerns I'd been grappling with the previous year were coming to a head, as if a cellar door had sprung open and unleashed those sub-terranean denizens into the light of day. I began to feel over-whelmed, and started shivering uncontrollably, my heart beating faster. Looking around, I even found myself wondering how I would climb down off of the boulder I was on without injuring myself, since I could no longer see the footholds I used to climb onto it.

As my anxieties snowballed, I decided to try and cope with them by slowing down my breath, in the hope that this would calm my mind. That helped slightly, and over the next few minutes the shivering lessened. But the turbulent emotions continued to well up every few moments, causing me to backslide into confusion and fear. In a last-ditch effort, I decided to simply surrender to the feelings rather than fight them, since resistance only seemed to make them worse. It was only then that they began losing their grip.

I then remembered something I'd heard on the car radio while driving towards the Canyon several days earlier, during an interview with a Japanese concentration camp survivor about the trans-forming power of love and forgiveness. That might hold a key for me now, I thought, as I began focusing my attention on love, on compassion—not just for others but for myself. My center of gravity slowly started shifting down from my head to my heart, and after about 10 minutes I felt vastly calmer, my breath dramatically slower, my anxieties gone.

With night starting to fall, I climbed down off the boulder, care-fully, and headed back to the campground. I felt relieved getting back to my tent, but I also felt as though something had shifted for me out there on the promontory.

That night I stayed up talking with some of the other camp-ers on the site. One of them was an acupuncturist named Joseph. Like me, he regarded his own trip through the Southwest as a personal vision quest of sorts, with the Canyon descent as the cornerstone of that experience. That sort of thing happens here a lot, apparently.

Roughly around eleven o'clock, I headed over to an outdoor water spigot provided for campers when out of the corner of my eye I saw a bright flash of light. I thought nothing of it at first, but then I heard a voice crying out, "*Help me!!! HELP ME!!!*" I looked over and saw the silhouette of a person flailing madly inside of a tent, its walls lit up from inside by a flickering mass of flames.

I rushed over towards the tent, exactly as a horde of other campers clamored out of the darkness towards the fire. I watched in horror as a young man emerged through a hole that had burnt through the side of the tent, as the man tripped over the fabric of the tent wall and fell hard onto the ground, his clothes smoking. I heard someone near me shouting, "He must have been using his stove in there. I smell fuel!"

The frantic young man picked himself up off the ground as sheets of melted flesh drooped down from his outstretched arms, creating a horrid stench that seared everyone's nostrils. Amazingly, he was perfectly ready to leap right back into the flames, since all he was concerned about was his camera and his backpack, which remained inside. From out of nowhere, a fellow camper appeared on the scene with a miniature fire extinguisher, and in a few moments put out the flames.

The situation jolted everyone into a state of adrenalized wakefulness, the atmosphere having become hyper-charged. The poor fellow looked seriously dazed, and the only thing he seemed able to say was, "How do I look? How do I look?" Just to calm him down, I said, "You look fine, you look fine." Just then, another camper walked up and said, gasping, "Jesus…you look terrible…"—which naturally threw the hapless fellow back into a state of full-blown anxiety.

A young female ranger in charge of the campground hurried onto the scene, and carefully escorted him back to the small cabin at the far end of the grounds. None of us standing around could really think about sleeping after all that commotion. After roughly 15 minutes, the ranger came back out to talk with us, saying she had no real medical supplies on hand and was concerned how the young man would fare once the shock wore off and the pain truly kicked in, burn wounds being what they are.

It was too dark to helicopter him out, she explained, so she asked if any of us had medical experience. When no one else stepped forward, the acupuncturist I'd spoken to earlier, Joseph, offered to see what he could do. He headed back to the cabin with her, but came back out a half hour later, saying the acupressure treatment didn't seem to make much difference. I'd dabbled in my 20s quite a bit with hypnosis, so I walked over and asked the ranger if she'd like me to give it a try, to see if I could help ease the man's pain? She seemed a little skeptical at first, but obviously had nothing to lose at that point, so she said, "Okay, follow me."

I stepped inside the cabin and saw the man seated in a chair, visibly shaking from discomfort. There was another camper standing alongside him, a bearded fellow named Ken who had some nursing experience. He was in the process of placing the young man's hands into a large bowl of ice water. The sight of his burnt arms under the bright light was sickening, almost as much as the stench. Ken took me aside and said they needed to apply medicinal gel to his arms before bandaging them up, but they were anxious about applying any pressure since it could make his pain worse. They had no painkillers anywhere on site, so if I could help bring the pain down even a little bit, that would help enormously.

I walked over to the fellow, and struck up a conversation, focusing on everything except the injuries so as to take his mind off of those. At first all he wanted to do was apologize over having done such a stupid thing outside. "I just wanted to cook some food, but I shouldn't have tried doing that in the tent like that, I know. I'm so sorry for causing everyone so much inconvenience, *I'm just so stupid...*" I tried to make light of the situation, and it was then that I learned his name was Rob and he was from a part of Illinois not far from my own home.

I had no set protocol for dealing with this sort of situation, so I was running on pure intuition. I kneeled down onto the floor and placed my left hand on the back of his head and began stroking his forehead with the fingers of my right hand, just to relax him. I told him to close his eyes and to slow down his breathing, which had been jerky and uneven up till then. I then gave him permission to let his body shake as much as it wanted, not to repress those feelings. That seemed to help a bit, since he'd been fighting those urges up to that point. After some initial violent shaking, he settled down considerably.

I felt a wave of compassion come through me, and it almost seemed as though I was pouring love through my hands into his body like a tangible energy. As I stroked his forehead, I sensed what he needed more than anything else was some caring and human touch, especially since he'd been so self-critical up to that point.

I started feeding him suggestions about how his hands and arms would grow numb, and that the healing powers of his own unconscious mind were now beginning to mend the wounds. I then took the risky step of telling him I was drawing the pain out of his body into my own. Whether or not that actually was taking place, the important thing was that he believed it—and at that point his shaking completely stopped.

I counted backwards from ten, telling him that when I reached zero, his hands would be completely numb, but that he would remain fully alert. When I reached zero, his face looked completely relaxed and peaceful. I then nodded to both the ranger and Ken, at which point the two of them now pulled his hands from the water and began applying gel across his arms. He initially felt a twinge of pain, but I gave him some more suggestions and the pain disappeared.

By the time it was over, twenty minutes later, his arms looked like two oversized Q-tips, the wrappings bunched up in thick wads around his hands. Both the ranger and Ken were worried over how he'd sleep that night, but after they walked him gently over to the side room and set him down on the cot, I kneeled down and once again gave him soothing suggestions, talking softer and softer, suggesting that he'd sleep soundly throughout the night, and wake up the next morning feeling completely refreshed. Before I'd finished, he was snoring loudly.

I walked quietly out of that room and back into the main office, and saw both the female ranger and Ken standing there staring at me. "That's the weirdest thing I've ever seen," Ken said. That made me feel self-conscious, so I just said goodnight and returned to my tent.

It was one o'clock in the morning by the time I climbed into my sleeping bag, reflecting on how unusual of a day it had been. Then it dawned on me how, in a way, Rob's struggle closely mirrored what I had gone through myself several hours earlier, with that anxiety attack I experienced out on the promontory. The suggestions I gave him for dealing with his own situation were the same as those I gave myself just hours before—slowing down my breath, cultivating love and self-acceptance, and not fighting the dark impulses. There was something synchronistic happening here, I thought.

The next morning, I stepped out from my tent to see Rob heading out to the promontory to be helicoptered out of the Canyon. He was glad to see me, and when I asked how he slept, he replied, "Like a baby! I didn't feel a lick of pain after the hypnosis. I still don't. It's amazing." I walked him out to where the helicopter landed, and waved goodbye as it whisked him up and away over the rim of the Canyon, as if by some hi-tech guardian angel. That's the last I ever saw of him.

After assembling my gear, I began my trek back up to the top of the Canyon rim. I was joined along the way by the acupuncturist from the night before, Joseph. On reaching the trailhead up top, we walked over to his car where he offered me some food and drink from the cooler in his trunk. I was ravenously thirsty, but when I took a few swallows from the cold beer he handed me, it hit my system so hard I nearly fainted, as the ground around me suddenly glowed white hot.

Shortly afterwards, I climbed into my car and headed north to Colorado.

CHAPTER 9

BOULDER

I came into town to meet up with my old friend and teacher from Chicago, Maura, who I hadn't seen in years. A Scorpio, she had been a major influence in my life during my early 20s. Apart from being my first astrology teacher, I was attracted to her unique combination of playfulness and stunning intelligence. While still in her mid-20s, she was teaching at the University of Chicago alongside such intellectual heavyweights as James Hillman, Paul Ricouer, and Mircea Eliade, among others—only to leave that all behind to become a full-time astrologer. We became friends during the time I studied with her, and at one point, became somewhat closer than just friends. But as those things go sometimes, we hit turbulent waters and drifted apart and didn't talk for years. Due to a highly unlikely chain of coincidences, our lives were crossing paths again, and I looked forward to seeing her.

Pulling up to her house, her two young children, who I'd never met before, greeted me like some returning war hero. Maura followed close behind with open arms and a smile that made it feel like no time at all had elapsed. Over the next few weeks the four or us would spend time talking, playing, and enjoying the scenic wonders around Boulder—including that strange experience with the dog high in the mountains.

I'd told her on the phone one week earlier that I also hoped to meet up with Chogyam Trungpa while in town. He was a well-known teacher in the spiritual community, and by most accounts a brilliant fellow with an insightful grasp of both Buddhism and Western psychology. Reading his books a few years earlier felt like a breath of fresh air to me compared to some of the other New Age literature clogging up the bookstore shelves during the 70s. Sitting in her backyard with the trees around us in bloom, she suggested I ask a fellow named John over at the Shambhala Bookstore about Trungpa. He was well-connected to Trungpa's organization and probably would know how to go about that.

The next morning I headed over to the bookstore to meet John. He was a man about my own age with longish hair and glasses, and when I informed him of my intentions, he raised one eyebrow and said, "Hmm...I don't want to discourage you, but that's nearly impossible. He hasn't met with anyone on a personal basis for months. Even a lot of his long-time students never get to meet him, you have to realize." That was disappointing, but I told him I'd like to try anyway. He suggested I write a letter spelling out my intentions, and if I did he promised to pass it along.

So that afternoon I sat down and started composing a letter to Trungpa, explaining how I was engaged in research that explored the symbolic and synchronistic dimensions of experience, and would appreciate getting his thoughts on these things from the Tibetan Buddhist viewpoint. As an afterthought, I decided at the last minute to include a photo of one of my paintings—the same one I gave to Percy on the Hopi Reservation. I knew Trungpa had an interest in art, so if my tactic with the painting worked in Hotevilla, maybe it will open doors for me here, too, I thought. After dropping the letter and reproduction off the next morning, I put the entire matter out of my mind so that I could spend the next couple weeks having fun with Maura and her kids.

A few days later I received a call from John from the bookstore. "Well, I have to admit I'm surprised, but it looks like Trungpa will meet with you after all. He thought your letter was impressive. I did too, I have to say. "But it wouldn't be a long appointment," he added, "probably only 10 or 15 minutes. But still, it's quite an honor, since he hasn't met with anyone outside the organization for months. Anyway, congratulations."

Meeting Trungpa

When the day arrived, I put on a suit jacket I bought from a second-hand store in town, trimmed my beard and moustache, and headed over to Naropa's administration building. I was told to wait over by two other individuals who were also scheduled for personal meetings and sitting patiently on a bench. The entire situation felt altogether too formal for my tastes, as if I were meeting with the Pope or a member of the Royal Family, but I was more than willing to play the game for this opportunity.

One of the attendants walked over and informed me of the protocol I should follow, explaining that I would have just ten minutes with him, and they'd knock on the door when my time was up. Soon, attendants ushered Trungpa down the hallway past us towards his room. He walked with a pronounced limp, the result of a car crash years earlier in England, and looked smaller than I expected. After a few moments, Beverly said softly, "You can follow me now." She led me into a side room where Trungpa was seated next to a table, with a glass of water placed next to a small vase containing a flower. The minimalistic room was sunlit, completely pristine and white, with very little decoration, and the overall ambience was one of bright silence. She said to Trungpa, "This is Mr. Grasse. He's the artist." I sat down at the chair next to the table and Beverly left us alone.

My first clear impression of Trungpa was that he looked like a fish. I don't know how else to put it. His facial features seemed vaguely aquatic, and there was a quality of delicacy and stillness to his demeanor. I introduced myself, turned on my tape recorder, and explained my reasons for coming to meet him. I dove right in and explained that I'm involved with studying synchronicity, or "meaningful coincidence," and how it relates to traditional concepts of fate, omens, and destiny.

"The basic premise of my book is that the outer and inner worlds are linked," I said. "In one of your own books you make a comment to the effect that outer events are 'decisive indicators of one's inner psychological state.' Is that correct?"

He answered in slow, quiet tones, and I was surprised to hear a vague British accent in his voice. "Yes, I believe that's true," he replied. "I think that is why there is always a chance for people to gain insight—the situation is always there, the opportunity for learning is always there, whether you are conscious of it or not. There's always a chance for everybody, because of the situations around them, always."

"Well, I'm wondering about that, because that idea has been so misunderstood or even abused by some in the New Age community that it concerns me. Tragedies are sometimes interpreted as saying you're somehow 'out of balance' spiritually, but worldly success indicates that you're 'in the Tao,' and that you're in tune with life. That seems frankly simplistic to me, and maybe even a little dangerous. So are you saying that the outer events and symbols in one's life are *exact* reflections of one's inner state? What about the 5-year old girl who is raped? Or if I contract cancer, does that mean I'm thinking 'cancerous thoughts'?"

He paused for a moment, then answered: "Yes, yes, well...I think you can't really talk very much about it. It's a question of experiencing it. If you begin to experience it, you look into it, and then you will experience it. That is the only way, and the words don't mean very much, you know...one has to experience it."

That answer was frustrating, because it frankly seemed more like a vague generalization than a real answer, perhaps even a cop-out. Rightly or wrongly, I felt that these things *could* be understood philosophically, especially in light of yogic mysticism and metaphysics, so I decided to press him further. I asked him if the answer ultimately tied in with karma, somehow.

"Well, yes, there is the whole matter of karma. Karma is the... *structure.* Sometimes there is harmony, and sometimes structure is in disharmony."

Sometimes structure is in disharmony—I understood that, or at least believed I did. What appears on the surface as messy can harbor a hidden order within it. That's an idea I'd been tinkering with for some time by that point. But I still wasn't sure if he was answering my question.

I mentioned to him that in the transcript to one of his lectures, he made the comment that "the universe is constantly trying to reach you to say something, it's teaching you something constantly, but you are rejecting it all the time." I liked that. But if there is some kind of message taking place, how does one go about *deciphering* that message, I asked?

"It's basically a matter of meditation…that will allow the situation to speak for itself naturally."

Hmm…A perfectly fine generalization, but is that really all one can say about it? After all, meditating 20 hours a day won't necessarily give you the ability to read German or Sanskrit. There's a rigorous learning process involved with *any* language, I thought, and I had to assume it's the same with reading signs and omens. It's fairly well known there were specific methodologies in the Tibetan tradition for interpreting signs and omens, or was I wrong about that?

"Well yes, there are texts…it's quite vast, actually. In those texts there are nine types of levels for understanding this. And each one of them involves a kind of training in order to perceive and understand properly. But most of those haven't been translated yet."

Now we were getting somewhere, I thought. "Will those texts ever be translated?"

"Well, we hope to work on them, some of them anyway. But a lot of them are lost, unfortunately."

I wanted to keep talking, and maybe ask some questions about spiritual practice, but before I knew it Beverly opened the door and said my time was up. I thanked him for his help, and he responded politely, "Thank you very much." I realized that in so short a session, I couldn't probe as deeply as I wanted, but I felt grateful at having the chance to talk with him at all. In some ways, it was even more interesting just sitting there and experiencing his presence as it was hearing his answers, since there definitely was something unique about him.

A Different Perspective

That night I made a phone call to Stan Brakhage, who lived just outside of Boulder. I hadn't spoken to him in a year, and wanted to catch up with him if possible. I mentioned in passing my experience with both Trungpa and the Naropa Institute, and it was obvious that I touched a nerve. He was involved with Trungpa's organization some years earlier as a result of his friendship with Allen Ginsberg, whom he'd known since the 50s (and who I saw at one point while studying at the Naropa library); but soon after that Stan came to distrust the organization, which he felt was repressive and dictatorial in its tactics.

"I could tell you some real horror stories. For one, they own the major bookstores in town, and so you'll never read a disparaging word about these things in Boulder. There are two books on the subject that touch on those horrors: *The Great Naropa Poetry Wars*, and *The Party*. But even these books couldn't include everything the authors wanted to. There's been some real bullying of people who aren't supportive of the organization. Yeah, Trunga is a sharpie of the first order.

"And as for Ginsberg—well, he's true to form," he added with a sigh. "He's always needed a guru, only they seem to get shoddier and shoddier."

He went on to tell me about an incident where some of Trungpa's underlings were supposedly caught breaking into an office to get their hands on magazine transcripts that were unfavorable to Trungpa. "What was so abominable about the whole thing was Ginsberg, really. He raised a stink over the Watergate cover-up, yet here he was defending this action by Trungpa's underlings when the story broke."

I was surprised to hear him make such critical remarks about Ginsberg, since years earlier I heard him speak in the friendliest terms about the poet, and years after this conversation I would hear him speak affectionately about Allen again. My sense was that they had a friendship that ran both hot and cold—and this period happened to fall on one of the chillier points on that arc.

After getting off the phone, I told Maureen about what Stan said, and she said she's heard most of these stories herself through the years. Why didn't she say anything to me beforehand? "I didn't want to color your meeting with Trungpa." That was wise, I thought, since it allowed me to come to my own conclusions about the man. I'd already heard some of those rumors myself, but it never really concerned me much since I was more interested in his knowledge than anything else. I've always believed one has to distinguish between a teacher and their teachings. And that seemed as true of Trungpa as anyone else. Besides, everything I was now hearing was second- or third-hand, so I couldn't make any final judgment about the man based just on that.

Paul Reps

One day before I was ready to leave town, I heard that a writer I'd long admired was going to speak at the Brillig bookstore in town that afternoon. Paul Reps was an American who was also an avid student of Zen Buddhism, and wrote a series of books about that tradition. The most famous of those was a short but cryptic book called *Zen Flesh, Zen Bones,* based on a series of longer and more complex Zen teaching tales from Japan and China. A few years earlier I heard Goswami Kriyananda refer to it as "one of the greatest books ever written," which certainly made me sit up and pay attention. The first time I tried reading it, though, it was like trying to decipher an alien language, the stories just seemed so strange and nonsensical. But as I went back and re-read the book several more times, the stories slowly started yielding up their insights and wisdom about the spiritual life.

Arriving at the bookstore, I took a seat with the others who were waiting for today's speaker. When he finally arrived, he smiled at the group then sat down without saying anything. He was short and bald, with a pleasant face that reminded me slightly of writer Henry Miller, who was roughly the same age and with whom he was sometimes compared (to his consternation, I discovered). Though he was almost 90, it was apparent that he was also extremely playful in spirit, and far beyond caring what anyone thought of him. The entire scene made for a dramatic contrast with what I encountered with Trungpa a few days earlier, since there was no entourage or bodyguards, no bureaucratic exoskeleton, and generally just no nonsense—just an old guy who seemed free as a bird.

His approach was unscripted and spontaneous, and it became obvious early on he was also quite the trickster. Moments after the gathering got underway he declared, "Okay, talk is over," smiling mischievously. Unlike many other public speakers, he wasn't afraid of long pauses during his talks. While everyone seemed to like his style, some didn't quite know what to make of him.

He asked someone seated several feet away from him, "Why did you come here today?" The man replied saying he was interested in hearing what the writer had to say. Reps pressed him, "Are you sure? You should check your ideas, your motives, your reasons. Because four out of five times they aren't what you think." It reminded me of Shelly Trimmer a bit, making the same point about always questioning one's own motives.

A few moments later Reps stopped in mid-sentence, as though he were listening carefully to a strange sound in the room, with a perplexing look on his face. "What *is* that?!" When a young woman pointed out that it was just an air conditioner, he said, as though springing a surprise on her, "Ah-hah! No, it isn't! I was alive and you were dead! You chose to put your conceptual ideas on it, by saying it was an 'air conditioner'!" His playfulness was obviously intended to awaken us out of our preconceived notions and prod us into seeing things afresh, but without getting too serious about it.

At one point he noticed that some of the people in the room were slumped over in their chairs, which prompted him to encourage everyone to sit up with their backs straight. "This is important in order for the feeling to come through us properly," he asserted. Up to that point, I was seated in a hunched-over position, legs crossed, taking notes. He pointed to me in particular and said, "Look at him—his posture, his self-wrestling! As long as he's seated like that, his heart or lungs can't operate effectively." Feeling immediately self-conscious, I shifted my posture. He asked all of us to stand up, lift our hands over our heads, then drop them down again.

He's having fun with us. There was a fellow sitting at a nearby table, reading through one of Reps' books, but seemingly oblivious to the aged teacher. The man was unshaven and his clothes untidy. Reps looked over and quipped, "You look like some kind of miner." He then commented on this fellow's bad posture, but none of it seemed to faze the young man. Reps had a way of delivering comments in such a humorously frank way that no one took offense. He kept talking in the man's direction: "Look at him reading; he's doing the impossible. How can he be reading and listening to me at the same time?" Without missing a beat, the fellow looked up and said, "I'm *not* listening." Everyone broke into laughter, including Reps. Reps eventually said to him, unexpectedly, "What *you* need is a *woman*...!" The man smiled slightly, then went back to reading his book.

Midway through the talk someone brought him a brush and paper and he began doing calligraphy. While applying the brush to paper, he referred in passing to the seeming contradiction of engaging in discipline while being spontaneous. I looked at him drawing his signature on the piece of paper before him, and he said he never drew his signature the same way twice in a row. When he was done, he held up the paper and cheerfully announced, "Okay, who bids the lowest!" Thinking I was pretty clever, I said aloud, "I'll give you nothing!" But another fellow next to me chimed in and went one better by saying, "You should pay *me* to take it!" Then the girl in the doorway managed to top both of us by saying, "I don't care whether you give it to me or not!" That got a good laugh out of Reps, who feigned indignation with a mock scowl. "Okay, who just *wants* it?" I quickly said that I did, as he reached over and handed it to me.

When the hour was over and he finished his presentation, I walked up to say how much I enjoyed his talk, but also to ask when he was born. "September 15th, 1895," he replied. That impressed me; I knew he must be up there in years, but considering his energy and vitality I would have guessed much younger. When he asked me why I wanted to know his data, I told him that I did astrology. To my surprise he said that he'd love to know what I saw in his chart, and that if I had time that evening, I should come by and tell him about it. But unfortunately, I already made plans with Maura and didn't want to renege on those, so I regretfully declined.

Early the next day, I said goodbye to Maura and her children, and headed back out on the road to Illinois. I felt exhilarated over what I'd experienced on this trip, but also deeply sad, as if a chapter was closing. The early morning light through the windshield was bright, and I lowered the visor to keep it out of my eyes. The sky stretched out before me looked vast, and the Rockies grew progressively smaller in my rearview mirror.

CHAPTER 10

"YOU ARE BRAHMA!"
AN ENCOUNTER WITH THE BODILY COSMOS

One afternoon a woman I knew who worked in the medical field told me excitedly about a unique technology she'd come across called *live-cell analysis*. "Normally, when you look at human cells under a microscope," she said, "they're already dead. Live-cell analysis allows you to look at your own blood cells while they're still alive."

I wasn't quite sure what the big deal was, but when she offered to demonstrate the technique for me next time I came into her office, I thought, Why not? What do I have to lose, other than a few drops of blood? So during my next visit to her workplace she drew a small blood sample from my finger and put it on a slide, then carefully placed it under a microscope. After adjusting the focus, she said, "Here, come take a look."

I shifted my chair over to where she had the microscope, squinted through the eyepiece—and proceeded to behold one of the most astonishing sights of my life. There, right before me, were thousands, possibly millions, of cells actively swimming around in plasmic fluid, all of them still alive, and all acting very much like miniature beings. Just moments earlier, that teeming population of cells had been inside my very own body, and here I was now watching them outside of me, struggling to survive, each one seemingly to have a certain sentience—possibly even individuality—of its own.

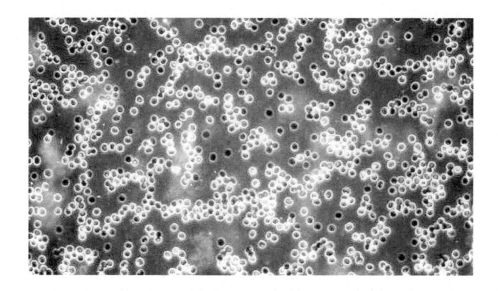

I'd read enough science articles by that point to know our body houses trillions of cells, but that meant almost nothing to me, since it was just an abstraction. But this time was different, since I could now actually *see* it. My body really *was* a cosmos of its own, embracing untold billions of living creatures all working in concert, vastly more numerous than the number of human beings living on Earth.

And this was all *inside of me.*

Making this even more startling was the fact that what I saw through that lens came from just the tiniest drop of blood. My imagination reeled at the thought of all the other cells in my body I *wasn't* seeing.

For days afterwards I felt a sense of awe over the magnitude of this body I'd always taken for granted. I became more conscious of my health, the effects of exercise, and of the foods and liquids I put into my body. Well, for a time, anyway. Ingrained habits being what they are, it wasn't long before I lapsed back into most of the old patterns I'd struggled with for years.

Still, the experience shifted my perception in significant ways, and fostered a sense of reverence for this vast network of minute creatures that comprise my body. I came to realize that I really was the steward responsible for their welfare, as it were, and that I needed to respect that responsibility and step up to the plate, no less than if I were a parent taking care of children. It's become a tired cliché hearing people refer to the human body as a "temple," yet that's exactly what this felt like to me. And what a monumental temple it was, when seen from the vantage point of the extremely small.

I was so taken with this discovery that I couldn't help but blather on about it for days to anyone patient enough to listen. One of those was my friend David Blair, a fellow student at the same yoga center I'd been studying at back then. When I described to him how striking this experience had been for me, seeing those millions of cells alive and which had come from my own body, he paused and said something that stopped me in my tracks:

"Just think, Ray: to all those cells, *you are Brahma!*" (In Hinduism, "Brahma" is one of the names for God.)

As offhand and light-hearted as that remark was meant to be, it triggered a shift in my mind that lifted my experience to another level. Because in that moment I realized that, in a way, I really *was* "God" to all those minute creatures swimming around in my body.

And that, in turn, caused me to wonder: What, exactly, is this "I," *this being* at the helm of it all?

It was a conceptual time-bomb, sparking a subtle awakening of who—or what—I was, as something formless yet radiant and endlessly mysterious. Dave was right: I truly was like some cosmic being compared to all those cells swarming around inside me. But that "I" wasn't localized in some specific part of my body, being more of a formless identity or ground awareness which encompassed and transcended it all.

Ever since that day, whenever I feel stalled in my contemplations, I think back to that comment, for which I'm indebted to my friend, the late David Blair. And each time I do, it triggers a similar awakening, however faintly, which reminds me of how remarkable this bodily universe—and its overseeing consciousness—is.

And I've never looked at a drop of blood spilled from a cut the same way again.

CHAPTER 11

ZEN MOUNTAIN MONASTERY

I arrived at the building's doorstep on April Fool's Day of 1986, with a small suitcase in tow. I'd read that this was an old-style Zen monastery, located in the Catskill Mountains of New York and housed in a large A-frame structure that once served as a Christian retreat for young people. I felt nervous standing at the entrance to the building, since I had so little idea of what to expect. For a moment, my anxiety became so great that I even contemplated turning around and driving back home. I'd studied with various spiritual teachers before but never in as intensive a setting as this. I now wondered whether I was really cut out for this kind of regimen.

Once inside, though, I was greeted by several friendly individuals who escorted me around the building and set my mind at ease. A few minutes later, the resident abbot, John Daido Loori, happened to pass through the office and introduced himself to me. An imposing but gentle presence, he was an American who served in the Navy for five years before entering the business world, only later becoming a Zen priest. Bald and fit, he appeared to be in his early 50s, and struck me as both gentle and rock-solid at the same time. He was warm and friendly to me, and the others at the center obviously treated him with respect.

The reason I had come there was simple enough. I'd been meditating for years but felt like I'd run into a brick wall. Though I'd had meaningful experiences in meditation here and there, my mind was usually so restless that sitting still for very long was always difficult. I grew convinced that mastering that stillness was an important step in taking my practice to another level. Signing on to the disciplined regimen of a center like this seemed like the best way to do that.

My second full day at the center, I was told I'd need to attend an introductory entrance interview, as all newbies do, where they are questioned about their reasons for coming to the center. Four of the senior students sat on the floor across from me, and only a minute or two into the proceedings I could see this was set up to resemble a "good cop/bad cop" arrangement, with two of the individuals looking stern and serious throughout while the other two appeared sympathetic, nodding appreciatively to all my responses.

They asked me a number of questions, but the primary one was simple enough: Why did I come there? My honest answer was, *I don't know*. I could have said any number of things, like wanting enlightenment or understanding myself better, and so on, but those would have been rationalizations. The bottom line is that I don't know why I do *anything*, let alone why I came there. Later on I learned that was considered a good answer in the context of Zen, though I never learned what they thought about the rest of my answers that day.

The next few months were a powerful learning experience, but not an easy one. The first 48 hours were especially difficult, since the schedule was so unlike anything I'd experienced before, and almost militaristic in its strictness. It felt at times like I had stepped into an alien world, but as I grew more familiar with the routine, I actually found myself liking it. *That* I didn't expect.

My first full day there, one of the senior monks sat me down to explain the routine they followed. For the better part of the week, each day would consist of three hours of meditation divvied up into three separate slots: one hour before breakfast, one hour after lunch, and then one more hour after dinner. Then, for one week out of the month, that pattern was extended into a formal *sesshin*, a long-term meditation marathon where students meditated anywhere from 7 hours to 14 hours, depending on the particular retreat. To my relief, I was told that every 35 minutes or so, meditators would be allowed to stand up and engage in a short five-minute walk, called *kinhin*. After that, we'd sit back down again to meditate for another period.

As it turned out, my first encounter with an all-day sitting led to one of the most humbling experiences of my life. At the start of the session, I sat down with my butt propped up on a cushion, but I decided to go for broke and cross my legs in full-lotus posture, each leg intertwined around the other. Normally, I can do that for up to ten or fifteen minutes without any problem. But I'd miscalculated my endurance this time, and after roughly 20 minutes I started to feel a stinging sensation in my legs, which grew more intense by the minute. I wanted to adjust my posture to lessen the pain, but since they strongly discouraged any movement during such sittings, that wasn't an option. (If you tried reaching up to scratch your nose during a sitting, say, the overseeing hall monitor loudly shouted out, "*Sit still!*" They don't fool around here.)

After about 30 minutes into the sitting, I realized that I'd lost almost all the feeling in my body from the waist down, other than that painful stinging. My legs were asleep, and when the bell finally rang to signal the end of the period, I became worried as to how I'd stand up and take part in the five-minute walking meditation. So whereas everybody else in the hall serenely rose to their feet, I struggled mightily to stand; but just as I reached an upright position, I started teetering precipitously over like a tree meeting the axe—and toppled backwards. I landed on the floor with a thunderous *BOOM*, the sound echoing throughout the otherwise quiet building. I was humiliated, but I eventually regained some feeling in my legs, along with a shred of my dignity, and rejoined the others in their walking meditation.

After the session, the overseeing monitor came up to me and graciously offered some advice about my meditation posture. She explained that I may have been sitting too low to the floor, and that I might try adding another cushion beneath me next time, to help prevent my legs from falling asleep. That turned out to be good advice, as I never ran into that problem again, not to that degree.

John Daido Loori

As I'd experienced with both Shelly and Goswami Kriyananda, Daido made no attempt to present himself as better than anyone else, and seemed perfectly ordinary in all his interactions with the others. But I could tell there was more that met the eye to that casual demeanor of his—a sense of grounded attentiveness that reflected his long years of meditating. He could lecture for hours on Zen when the occasion called for it, but the teaching I remember most of all from him was perhaps the simplest:

"You live your life in the moment. Miss the moment and you miss your life."

He was roughly the same age as Kriyananda, and there were some other parallels. Like Kriyananda, he too lost his father at a very young age, had a stint in the military, and both of them spent years working in the professional world as a chemist. One chief difference was Daido's intimate involvement with the arts, having been an accomplished photographer earlier in life, and emphasizing "art practice" as an important activity amongst students at the monastery. In fact, he first got interested in Zen through his studies with the famed photographer Minor White, who exposed him to meditation, chanting, and breathing techniques. Indeed, it was White's astrologer who told him he would eventually become involved with spiritual teaching and writing books. Upon being told that, he was incredulous.

"I laughed hysterically. I told her, 'Lady, you have no idea how wrong you are. I'm an atheist! I hate religion!' She said, 'No, no— that's what you're going to be doing, many years from now. And this is all preparation for that.'"

In one of the books he eventually did write, he said, "I trust zazen because I was probably the most deluded, confused, angry, anti-religious person you could ever meet. There is no reason in heaven or hell why I should be a Zen teacher, sitting here, talking like this. All I know is I found out about zazen." ("Zazen" is, simply put, sitting meditation as practiced in the Zen tradition.)

He had grown up in a rough-and-tumble neighborhood of New Jersey, and saw myself that he could be tough—well, *firm* is a better word—in running the monastery and its activities. He essentially struck me as kind-hearted, and his human side sometimes showed itself in unexpected ways. Like the fact that he still smoked cigarettes—a habit which eventually took its toll. Another way was the amusing fact he made no bones about not being terribly fond of the vegetarian cuisine at the monastery, preferring to eat at the truck stop down the road on occasion. I had the feeling he did that as much for spiritual reasons as culinary ones, opting for the gritty ordinariness of the truck stop as a counterbalance to the surreal austerity of the monastery. I say that because I once asked him directly about his philosophy of diet, and he replied how one should "taste a little bit of everything," and it was obvious he meant that as much a philosophy of life as a dietary guideline.

John Daido Loori: Photograph by Stuart Soshin Gray

There were also instances of his vulnerability, and some of those were deeply touching. During one meditation retreat, Daido was delivering his customary *dharma talk*—a lecture meant to motivate and inspire students in their practice—and recounted an ancient Japanese tale of forbidden love, centering around a young man and woman who encountered assorted obstacles in their efforts to share their love. Although it was just a fictional morality tale, it was a deeply moving one, and by story's end Daido became so choked up with emotion that he stopped talking and blushed a shade of red so intense I could see it from across the darkened meditation hall. I'd never seen him that emotional before, as compassionate laughter among the students began rippling through the hall. Rather than make anyone feel uncomfortable, his vulnerability evoked great affection from everyone present—especially those of us who knew about the personal heartache he experienced several years earlier when his wife left him for another Zen practitioner at the center.

Monastery Life

My stay at the monastery unfolded in two separate visits. The first of those took place in the Spring, as a kind of month-long trial run, after which I came back in the Fall and Winter for just under four months. During the bulk of my time there, I lived in a make-shift cabin up on a nearby hill, along with two other students. Our sleeping spaces in that small structure weren't so much "rooms" as cubicles separated by plywood partitions. It wasn't always easy sharing our space; I was awakened on more than one occasion by one of my roommates thrashing about in the throes of night terrors. I never learned what demons were tormenting him, or what drove him to monastic life in the first place; there may well have been a connection between those. But he seemed normal and well-adjusted enough during his waking hours. During the winter months, we'd make our way by flashlight down the snowy rocky path to the monastery to begin our pre-dawn meditations. I've never been much of an early morning person myself, but I grew accustomed to the routine relatively soon.

Zen Mountain Monastery is structured along co-ed lines, which means that both men and women partake in its programs. That's probably the biggest difference between the center and its Japanese counterparts. From an egalitarian standpoint that's probably a good thing, but on a more practical level it poses its own set of problems, something I discovered myself. It's not easy focusing on your meditation when you're seated next to someone you find attractive and your mind starts dallying in sensual fantasies.

I spoke once with Daido about that problem, and he recalled the time some monks from an all-male monastery came from Japan as part of an exchange program between the centers. The visiting monks were highly disciplined meditators, but what their previously cloistered lifestyle hadn't prepared them for was the rather casual dress codes of American women attending these stateside retreats. During off-hours on summer weekends, some of the younger women would lie out in the sunlight in their skimpy outfits, which apparently made meditating especially difficult (dare I say "hard"?) for the visiting monks. Because they'd never been exposed to women much at all—let alone to women that exposed—they could barely contain themselves.

Considering all the attractive females that came through the doors of the center during my own stay there, I asked Daido whether he ever found that to be a problem himself. He said, frankly, "No. During my five years in the Navy, I screwed my way through South America, so I got it out of my system. Those monks from Japan never did."

Most of the fellow students I crossed paths with at the center seemed serious and sincere, but some were clearly more serious and sincere than others. One was an especially earnest student named Geoffrey "Shugen" Arnold, a young man in his late 20s who was clearly fervent about his spiritual practice. When he eventually became a leading figure in the community, which I later heard, it didn't surprise me at all. Another was Bonnie "Myotai" Treace, a sensitive and intelligent 30-something with an English degree who spoke openly about her earlier stint as a stripper in Texas back when she had to support her baby after a divorce.

During my time there, Myotai seemed close to Daido, and at one point it became clear their friendship had become romantic. Although they didn't flaunt their relationship, most of us knew what was going on. Personally, it didn't bother me in the slightest, not only because it seemed like a genuinely loving, monogamous relationship but because Myotai struck me as a strong, independent person who knew what she was doing so there was never a sense of one person taking advantage of another. Since that time, I've since read at least one critique of Daido on the Internet questioning whether it was proper for him to become romantically involved with a student that way. Since I was present when their relationship happened, I feel inclined to weigh in on the matter.

It was clear to me that Daido was a person of integrity, and not at all inclined to abuse or "sleep around" with women in the community—unlike quite a few other, less honorable teachers working the spiritual circuit. I also think it's also worth pointing out Daido's life revolved entirely around the monastery, so there wasn't much chance of him meeting women outside that environment, so I felt a certain empathy for his situation. There's no question that critics raise an important point when they talk about the risks of a teacher becoming involved with a student, due to the potential problems that can arise—emotionally, spiritually, even legally. But personally, I didn't see any of those problems arising in the relationship between Daido and Myotai. Okay, let's move on.

As for the larger community at the monastery, virtually all of the men and women I encountered there were easy to relate to, but as in any group there are always some personalities who will grate on your nerves, and I had to deal with a few of those myself. That's probably a good thing, actually, since difficult people keep you on your toes. Just when you start to think you have it all together, along comes an abrasive personality who shows you just how wrong you really were.

Aside from sittings or workshops, the weekends were relatively free, and every Sunday night a few of us would congregate in the small library upstairs to watch movies on video. Knowing my background with film back in college, Daido put me in charge of selecting videos from the local video store down the road for those weekend screenings. Not everyone was happy with my choices, I soon realized, since I veered towards more "artsy" selections rather than more familiar crowd-pleasers. Nonetheless, it was one of the more enjoyable social activities at the monastery, since it gave students a chance to spend time together in a casual setting.

Daido and I shared a love of movies. Whenever he had the time, especially on weekends, we knew that Daido watched movies on video cassettes that he rented from that same small video store I'd frequent. His own choice of viewing matter was surprisingly eclectic, and ranged from action films to romantic comedies and art house films, as well as, of course, spiritually-oriented movies. On one occasion, that fondness for film led to an exchange that revealed yet another facet of his life and personality.

Some of us were in the kitchen cleaning up after dinner, when a fellow student teasingly said to Daido, "Hey, aren't all those movies you watch just an escape from reality?" Daido paused a second, then said, lightheartedly but not without purpose: "Hey...I get enough reality in the dokusan room. . ." The "dokusan room" was the small interview room off from the main hall where Daido would sit face-to-face with individual students ostensibly to discuss problems they were having with their meditation practice, or to discuss some other spiritual matter. But those encounters with students could become intense sometimes, judging from the sounds of crying I sometimes heard through the door to the room as I waited outside. It's entirely possible those sounds may well have been due to tears of joy resulting from breakthroughs in their meditative practice, but just as often I suspect it was because of how some students approached those interviews more like therapy sessions. And his comment in the kitchen that day told me something very important—namely, that even the most elevated spiritual teachers need some sort of "escape," some creative outlet to let off steam. In Daido's case, he had a hefty burden of responsibility on his shoulders overseeing the monastery and its residents, and it was obvious that movies were a key release valve for him.

Out for a walk with fellow monastery student, 19-year old Ray Bonini.

As for my own release valve—I would sometimes go on hikes through the adjoining mountains, or drive into Woodstock for the afternoon with a fellow student or two, past Bob Dylan's old home a few miles down the road. But I increasingly spent the bulk of my free time working on my writing projects. I'd put *The Waking Dream* temporarily on hold to spend time working on a "sequel" of sorts, which I tentatively titled *History as Dream*. I was pleasantly surprised to discover Daido was supportive of my writing, not so much because of the topic itself but because of the intellectual discipline involved. I came to the monastery armed with certain misconceptions about how Zen Buddhists regarded mental activity of any kind, but Daido was careful to point out that Buddhism doesn't think thoughts are inherently bad, only that unwise attachment to them can be—a point both Kriyananda and Shelly repeatedly made as well. To drive home the point about the importance of "right thought," he told the following story.

Several years earlier during a brutally cold winter, some of the local residents thought they'd perform a good deed for the nearby wildlife, since it looked as though the local deer population might starve from a lack of food. A few of the townspeople banded together and paid to have a helicopter drop bales of hay onto a spot where the deer could find it. Just as expected, the deer did find it—but not so expectedly, they all died. The reason? Their stomachs had acclimated to eating bark off of the local trees and weren't able to digest the hay as a result. As Daido explained, that illustrated how using compassion without also using the mind can lead to bigger problems than one began with.

Critical Mass

From the beginning, I was encouraged to start with a simple meditation technique in order to learn their particular system from the ground up. There were several different techniques I could choose from, but for most beginners, simply focusing one's attention on the breath or silently counting one's exhalations were recommended points of departure. So that's where I got my start.

My meditation unfolded in fits and starts. There were days when I felt focused, but other days when my mind seemed completely out of control. Despite the fact that we were told not to fall into the trap of judging our meditation as either "good" or "bad," and that we should take each sitting on its own terms, that's hard when you're experiencing such extreme highs and lows. I found it encouraging to learn that even some of the advanced students there sometimes had trouble sitting in meditation for extended periods. But there can be real breakthroughs sometimes, when everything seems to fall into place. One of those, a small one, occurred for me during my second week there.

It was the last hour of an all-day meditation period, and I had begun to feel like I was stuck in a rut. The sun had just set and the sounds outside had grown quiet, as the sensation of my breath rushing in and out became subtly more pronounced. My mind was restless, and the sensations in my legs had become painful again so I decided, almost out of desperation, to pour every last drop of energy into the meditation technique itself, largely to escape from the discomfort. The pain in my legs worsened by the minute. Throughout the day I'd been counting my breaths silently, while staring down on the floor, as I was instructed to do. But now I began throwing my whole being into the technique, zeroing in like a laser beam on my breath, the counting, and the floor, all at once, in hope of breaking through the pain.

Then, after a few minutes, something surprising happened: *I simply became present.* I left behind the past, as well as expectations about the future, and I was simply there in the moment. No desire or grasping, just pure contentment with what was.

And with that, the previously ordinary floor became extraordinary, luminous and vibrant, as an indescribable sense of peace flooded through me. The tremendous discomfort I'd been feeling up to that point immediately vanished as if having been turned off like a switch—and my entire being exploded into a radiant field of light. The sensation was so palpable that I felt sure anyone looking in my direction would have seen visible waves of light emanating from my body. It was pleasurable beyond words, and even the thought of sex paled by comparison, amazingly. More importantly, though, there was a peacefulness about it unlike anything I'd experienced before. Shelly used to talk about the "peace that goeth before all understanding"—and I was getting a very tiny taste of that now. I sat in that condition for another 10 minutes or so, marveling at what was going on, until the bell rang to signal an end to the period, as I walked out of the hall feeling overwhelmed with joy.

During my next private interview with Daido, I described what happened and he verified that it was a rudimentary level of *samadhi*, or effortless one-pointed absorption. But it wasn't enlightenment, to be sure, just a useful stage in my practice. He was also careful to add that I shouldn't become attached to the experience, let alone try to recreate it. As I continued deepening my meditation, he said, that sense of joy would probably become even stronger, but joy wasn't so much the goal as simply a by-product.

The intoxicating high I felt in the wake of that experience lingered for days. The next morning, while standing outside in the snow chopping wood along with some of the others, I looked up towards the blue sky at one point and noticed the sunlight on my face, and felt a sense of deep happiness. After a few days, that feeling faded and by the next week it was just a faint afterglow, but lingered in a more subtle way.

I've given a lot of thought to that experience since then, trying to make sense of what happened, and I came up with an analogy: a phenomenon referred to as "critical mass." That's a term astrophysicists use to describe what happens when a chain reaction takes place amongst a collection of atoms, and energy is released from out of a previously dense mass of matter. Under the pull of gravity, for example, a massive dust cloud floating in space will coalesce into ever larger clumps, and over time become so tightly compressed that a chain reaction takes place, called "fusion"—and the energy trapped in that matter transmutes into light. Quite literally, *a star is born*.

In a way, samadhi must be like that. In that state, awareness becomes so tightly focused that the inherent light-energy concealed within it breaks open—and the meditator goes super-nova, as it were. For so much of our lives, our consciousness is frittered away on trivia rather than on the direct experience of the moment; but in samadhi, that evasive maneuvering stops and we suddenly look at what is *right here, right now*—and in that looking, everything becomes alive and bright, and real.

I've come to think that's a good part of the reason why some people engage in daredevil activities like skydiving or mountain climbing, because they offer a way to evoke a similar kind of awakening. By dancing close to the edge, one is forced to become completely focused in the present—and the result is a natural high. Part of that is pure adrenaline, no doubt, but part of that also has to do with a state of heightened awareness. But it naturally begs the question: does one really have to risk life and limb to attain that? Or can it be attained in far simpler way, such as when one is pouring a cup of tea? Or watching one's breath? Or taking out the garbage?

During the next few months or even years, I'd experience other meaningful moments in meditation, but none quite like that. A year later I came across a passage by Marcel Proust that summed up what I felt that day: "The real voyage of discovery consists not in seeking new landscapes, but in having new eyes." I knew if I could find it in a wooden floor, like I did that day, I could find it anywhere, if I was open and focused enough.

Leaving the Monastery

It was in early 1987 that I decided to leave the monastery and return to the Midwest. It was tempting to remain at the center, since all my basic survival needs would be met with little or no chance of starving or getting evicted, as might happen out in the real world.

But for me, that was part of the problem. It felt to me like remaining there would have been an escape. That may not have been true for any of the others there, but it was for me; I had some real-world lessons I still needed to learn, I knew, and had to confront them. I'd dealt with so many setbacks and feelings of failure those previous years that staying at the center would have been the easy way out. I had to prove something to myself.

The morning I left, I packed up my car and made the several hour drive into Manhattan, where I'd meet up with a young couple I first met at the monastery who offered to put me up for the night.

On getting up the next morning to drive out of the city, I walked outside to discover that the rear passenger window of my car had been shattered and most of my belongings gone. A wave of dread flooded through me as I realized that among the missing items was the bag containing the manuscript I'd spent the last half-year working on. It contained roughly 300 finished pages of a projected 450-page book—and all that was gone now. I'd made a back-up copy for protection, but that was in the car, too, and had disappeared along with the original. After searching fruitlessly through the neighborhood for any trace of my belongings, hoping the thief might have tossed the unwanted items in a nearby trash can or alley, I staggered back to my car and began driving back to Illinois, shell-shocked and numb.

As it so happens, I'd spent some time over the previous week reading an essay on the Buddhist doctrine of impermanence, and the challenge of realizing how nothing in life lasts forever. But as I was now discovering, it's one thing to contemplate that idea as an abstract philosophical principle, quite another coming to terms with it in everyday life. That proved to be a different challenge altogether—and an excruciatingly hard one.

CHAPTER 12

THE WAKING DREAM

The seeds first planted in my brain by my encounter with the Hermetic writings—and the axiom *As Above, So Below,* in particular—continued to unfold through the years, watered along the way by influences like astrology, mythology, yogic philosophy, and others. But they experienced a special growth spurt when I finally came across the concept of "synchronicity."

In one form or another, I'd always been fascinated by unlikely coincidences, and while growing up I paid special attention to stories about them whenever they cropped up in the news. Like the newspaper story about a would-be-thief who walked into a Chicago bank hoping to cash a phony check. He signed it using an assumed name—only to discover that the name he picked randomly out of the phone book belonged to the husband of the female bank teller in front of him. The article closed with a comment from the officer in charge saying that the last time he looked in on the offender, he was sitting in his cell staring off into space, obviously blindsided by the interlocking gears of fate.

But it wasn't until freshman year at the Art Institute of Chicago that I discovered there actually was a term for those mysterious occurrences: *synchronicity.* Unlike Stan Brakhage, a staunch Freudian and decidedly *non*-metaphysical, my other film professor, John Scofill-Luther, was a staunch Jungian and explained how the Swiss psychologist coined this term to describe the way some coincidences hinted at a deeper meaning, as though they were involved in a larger pattern of connectedness. "Perhaps the universe isn't quite as random as we think," John said with a smile.

And so it was shortly before my 30th birthday, and just months before my trip through the Southwest, that I conceived of writing a book on this topic, which I decided to call *The Waking Dream*. The deeper I delved into this subject, the more I found myself diverging from Jung's perspective in several ways.

Rather than see synchronicity as a relatively rare phenomenon, as Jung did, I came to see that "coincidences" were actually *pervasive* throughout our lives, in a wide variety of ways. Astrology drove that point home for me with special force, since it showed how the diverse phenomena of our daily life—from people and objects to random events—were interconnected through a network of correspondences, with the rare and obvious coincidence being only the tip of a larger iceberg of interconnectedness. Said a little differently, everything is a coincidence in that *everything co-incides.*

Alongside that was another of the book's themes, that the events in our lives can be interpreted much in the same way as our nightly dreams—in other words, as *symbolic events.* There's a close connection between what's happening outside of us and the psychological changes taking place inside of us. Or, to flip the old Hermetic axiom around slightly, *As without, so within.* One of the aims of my book would be to illustrate how this perspective could be applied to an assortment of situations in our lives—relationships, life challenges, spiritual practice, omens, and so forth—using insights drawn from the traditions and teachers I'd studied under along with my own observations. Besides presenting a revision of Jung's synchronicity concept, this would also be a book on learning to read the language of life experience.

But the book's focus kept expanding, and morphing from a relatively short meditation on coincidence and symbolic events into something considerably broader: a synthesis of various symbolic systems. I'd come across a wide range of esoteric concepts and systems over the years, which included astrology, sacred geometry, alchemy, ritual, karma, archetypes, the chakras, correspondences, and of course, synchronicity. But the longer and deeper I looked into these, the more I saw subtle linkages connecting them, and how they could be integrated within an overarching framework. I termed that framework *symbolist* (after the esoteric scholar Schwaller de Lubicz).

After experiencing a spell of writer's block with that book during the mid-1980s, I turned my attention to the other work I'd been tinkering with for some years, *History as Dream;* but after the heartbreaking loss of that manuscript in New York City, I couldn't bring myself to resume work on it and decided to go back to *The Waking Dream.* The writer's block had ended, and in 1989 I felt like the pieces might finally be coming together.

After working for a year at a resort in Tucson, Arizona called Canyon Ranch, I returned to Illinois in hope of reviving a failed relationship with my old partner (and soon-to-be wife) Judith. Those first few months back in Illinois were difficult, and saw me working the graveyard shift at United Parcel Service through the winter months, where I became a card-carrying member of the Teamsters Union. I sorted mail on a platform directly above a row of parked delivery trucks, where I inhaled exhaust fumes throughout the night. Early each morning I'd return home from work with a migraine headache and nausea, all triggered by those hours of inhaled truck fumes. I knew this couldn't go on much longer.

Largely out of desperation, I applied for work at the Theosophical Society just a few miles down the road in nearby Wheaton. I'd attended lectures and workshops there since my mid-20s, the first of those with astrologer Dane Rudhyar, and always liked what they stood for and promoted. But I never seriously considered applying for work there, due to the low wages, which is a pretty standard reality for non-profit organizations, especially spiritual ones. But now my sanity and health were on the line, and I was willing to consider anything, no matter what the pay.

The Theosophical Society in America
I began in a low-level position—basically putting stamps on envelopes—and slowly moved my way up the organizational adder. I

had no background in editing, but I'd read a great deal, and wound up being invited to help with editing and acquisitions for both the magazine and book divisions—Quest Magazine and Quest Books. Financially, it was difficult since I made only five dollars an hour during my first five years there, and butted heads with some of the board members who regarded me as an "outsider" of sorts, not part of the Theosophical inner circle.

The Olcott Library at the Theosophical Society in America, Wheaton

But it was an extraordinary opportunity in many ways. For one, there were the fascinating writers and artists I came to connect with, like Richard Tarnas, Gary Lachman, Ken Wilber, Jean Houston, John David Ebert, Georg Feuerstein, Catherine Ingram, Stephan Hoeller, Rand Flem-ath, Richard Heinberg, David A. Cooper, Judith Cornell, Andrew Harvey, Joan Halifax, Stephen Levine,

Jack Kornfield, Glenn Mullin, Michael Grosso, David Frawley, John Anthony West, Alex Grey, and my dear friend Normandi Ellis, among others.

There were some truly surprising encounters along the way, too. A few of us on the staff were involved with organizing the Parliament of World Religions held in Chicago in 1993, a mammoth undertaking that involved coordinating religious figures and groups from around the world. Like its predecessor a century earlier in 1893, the aim was to stimulate a dialogue amongst the world's various faiths, hopefully culminating in a joint statement by the various speakers promoting greater political and religious harmony throughout the world. There was a sense of electricity in the air amongst the attendees, since this was a chance to mingle with others of like mind or encounter well-known teachers like Swami Satchitananda or Amma, the "hugging saint." The main activities of the Parliament were held at Chicago's Palmer House hotel. While I attended as many talks as possible, the one I was most drawn to was a press conference convened by the Dalai Lama.

As usual, His Holiness's comments were inspiring and noble, concerning the need for harmony amongst countries and peoples, and all that. But frankly, one doesn't usually go to hear the Dalai Lama for his words so much as for his non-judgmental, compassionate presence. The modest ballroom where he spoke was packed, standing room only, with roughly 300 people in attendance, many of them from the media. My boss at the magazine, Bill Metzger, was seated in the front row while I stood off to the side several feet away. It had been a rough week for Bill, since his wife was in the last stages of cancer and given only weeks to live. He was able to break away for just a few hours to attend this gathering, and it was obvious he felt relieved to have a little time off from his caretaking responsibilities.

The moment the press conference ended, the Dalai Lama darted from his podium and rushed over to Bill, clasping Bill's hands fervently and uttering something to him (which neither of us later recalled)—and then, just as quickly, throngs of admiring men and women rushed in to touch the proverbial hem of the holy man, as the Dalai Lama disappeared into a sea of outstretched arms. I was struck by the fact that out of the hundreds of people in the room, the Dalai Lama zeroed in on *Bill*, who was going through such a terrible time. Nor was Bill the nearest audience member to him at the time; he wasn't. It may have been just a coincidence, but one hears stories like that in association with spiritual teachers quite often, in terms of their seemingly heightened awareness of others' suffering.

Then there were the booksellers' conventions during the 1990s where I'd join up with a few co-workers to oversee the Quest Books' booth each year to display our latest publications. Gatherings like that are generally a nightmare for introverts, since you're dealing with hundreds of people every hour while being bombarded with sensory stimuli from every direction. But they can also make for some interesting encounters. Besides running into figures like James Hillman, Timothy Leary, and Mickey Hart, I remember one bookseller's convention where a youngish man came by our booth to tell us about an online bookselling company he'd recently founded. That seemed like a strange idea to me; but then, the internet seemed like a strange idea to me then too. I took his card and talked it over a little with my co-workers, then essentially forgot about him. It was nearly 20 years later while cleaning out my file cabinets that I came across his business card; the young man had been Jeff Bezos.

But the most meaningful encounter for me of all during those years took place one afternoon back at the Theosophical headquarters in Wheaton. While walking through the hallway I saw a Hispanic man with two other gentlemen alongside him walking into the building's lobby, where there are displayed beautiful murals featuring esoteric themes from decades past on its walls.

The three men were looking up at the murals, and it was obvious this was their first time there. The shorter man in the middle looked vaguely familiar, but I couldn't place his face. One of my co-workers came up and whispered to me, "That's *César Chávez!*" My friend was right. It turned out the dark-haired fellow was the famed activist and migrant worker organizer who gained fame during the 60s as the "Hispanic Martin Luther King." Someone passed word back up to the current president of the Society, Dorothy Abbenhouse, who came down from her office, and for the next fifteen minutes we stood around talking with César and his two companions. I asked what drew him to the building, and he replied, "I've long been interested in the Society's publications." I knew from his background he was a courageous and gutsy individual, yet during that conversation he seemed extremely soft-spoken and humble.

During the early 1990s, both Quest magazine and Quest Books became leading voices in the New Age or "alternative spirituality" movement. There was a feeling of excitement in the air throughout this period, when new ideas and technologies began appearing on the scene in various areas. As an astrologer, I chalked that up to the rare alignment of Uranus with Neptune that was in effect during that decade, and opening up new horizons in the culture. A new crop of journals and publications devoted to spiritual topics also began emerging, like *Common Boundary, Intuition, Parabola, Magical Blend, Tricycle,* and *Yoga Journal.* But the general consensus was that *The Quest* and its rival publication in California, *Gnosis,* were the cream of the crop. Judging from the letters and comments which came our way, each new issue was anticipated by readers in a way that would become hard to understand in the later era of the Internet, when thought-provoking essays and news items would become a dime a dozen, all free for the taking. But times were different then, and we felt as though we were seeding new ideas into the emerging cultural ferment.

The Book

In the end, though, the most creatively rewarding aspect of this period concerned the publication of my book. There seemed to be more than a little synchronicity in how things were coming together for me with that project. In addition to the Theosophical Society's library, which afforded me access to a gold mine of information that proved invaluable for my research, it often happened where I'd be searching for an obscure quotation or piece of information only to find it in a book that arrived in the mail that morning for review in our magazine. So as difficult as this period was for me other ways, it nonetheless felt like hidden hands were helping me finish the book. It certainly had been a long time coming; from when I began writing it in the early 1980s, the book had gone through probably 70 drafts in all.

Finally, in the spring of 1996 Quest Books published *The Waking Dream*. I'd submitted it to a number of publishers, but the Theosophical Society were the ones who offered me a contract. As every author knows, holding that initial copy of one's first work is a magical experience, something you never experience in quite the same way again. But it can also be deeply unsettling, since you feel incredibly vulnerable and exposed, as though your soul were being laid bare before the world. My own experience was tempered by the fact that I had to make some painful concessions with the lead editor about the book, which included an insistence that I lessen its emphasis on synchronicity, both in the book's introduction as well as on the book's cover. They felt the concept's obscurity would hurt sales. As it turned out, "synchronicity" became a buzzword in the publishing industry those next few years, propelling nearly every book with that word on its cover into stellar sales territory. Well, you win some, you lose some.

There were a couple of negative reviews, but the vast majority were positive. The very first one was written by Gary Lachman for *Gnosis* magazine. Perhaps the most uplifting (and unexpected) feedback came in the form of a phone call I received while at work one day. The receptionist on the intercom informed me there was a long-distance call on line three. I picked up the phone, and the man on the other end said, "Hello, this is Colin Wilson. I'm calling from England, and I just want to say I think you've written a masterpiece." Here was a writer whose work I'd been reading for years, so hearing him say that left me feeling exhilarated for days.

It was around that time I started reflecting on the curious chain of circumstances that led up to the book's publication. My life up to that point had been largely a succession of professional and creative detours, false starts, and cul-de-sacs, like those which happened for me with painting, writing and filmmaking. I had an especially heartbreaking setback in 1979, when I applied for a job at Francis Coppola's studio complex in San Francisco, Zoetrope, during post-production work on *Apocalypse Now*. I'd moved out there hoping I had landed a position working as an apprentice under Walter Murch on the film's sound mix—only to learn at the last minute that the position had been given to someone else. There were other disappointments besides those. But I came to realize my book wouldn't have come together as it did had things worked out any differently for me early on, since I almost certainly wouldn't have wound up working at the Theosophical Society when and how I did—which proved an indispensable stage in my writing and editing career. I learned more from reviewing and editing the thousands of manuscripts that came across my desk during that period than I would have under virtually any other circumstance. When Kriyananda did my horoscope in my early 20s and told me I was a late bloomer and things would start to unfold for me when I got older, I hoped he meant that would be sometime in my 30s. I'm not sure I would have been too happy had I known that would actually prove to be closer to my mid-40s.

There was also something fitting about how so many of those earlier creative pursuits—including those which originally seemed like dead-ends—fed into the completion of this book in ways I couldn't have foreseen. My background in painting and drawing helped conceive the layout of the book, both with the inside illustrations and the outside cover art; my background in film informed some of the cinematic examples I used; I even suspected my early training in music forged neural pathways that made me more aware of correspondences and synchronicities in the world than I would have otherwise. It reminded me of that passage from Schopenhauer which Joseph Campbell liked to quote—namely, how when seen in hindsight one's life can appear like a carefully constructed novel, with the seemingly unintended events along the way turning out to be integral components of a larger unfolding destiny. I was beginning to see my own life that way now.

The book never racked up blockbuster sales, but it did well enough to be translated into several languages and spawn a few copycat books on synchronicity and symbolism by other authors. For a number of years, I continued getting scattered feedback from readers or friends, some of which was surprising. My friend Thea called from Bali where she was vacationing with her husband Larry to let me know they walked into the small library of their five-star hotel and found my book prominently displayed on its main shelf. Then there was the email I received from a professor at the Digipen Institute of Technology in Washington State, a modest-size technical school specializing in video game design. He wrote to say he made my book required reading for his students, and wanted to order a large number of copies. Why my book, I wondered? Because he thought it would "give them a good background in symbolic thinking and archetypal imagery when conceiving new games." I was intrigued to think that ideas I penned for a book on philosophy might someday filter their way into video games kids could be playing years from now. It just goes to show you never really know what life your children will take on once they've been released out into the world.

CHAPTER 13

BURIED TREASURES
UNCOVERING THE LOST TOMB OF OSIRIS

*P*relude: *The Sun breathes a golden hymn across the land on days like this. Every grain of sand seems to glisten as I approach the cave-like entrance nestled into the side of the causeway, which stretches out from the Great Pyramid to my left towards the Sphinx over on my right. I've been looking forward to this moment for months already, and after grappling these last few years with a multitude of personal problems, I'm excited at the prospect of becoming involved with what looks to be an important archeological discovery. Making my way down the rusty metal ladder bolted into the sides of the stone walls of the shaft, it feels to me as though each step down is*

transporting me back further in time, to an era and a culture thousands of years older than my familiar one. This is the heart of the Giza Plateau, and I'm here to partake in an investigation that will explore a mysterious chamber at the bottom of an abandoned well-shaft, 100 feet underground. This partially flooded chamber has been a source of speculation for decades, and news of this expedition has been spreading like wildfire across the internet in recent months. What was down here, exactly? And what was its original function? These are some of the questions that members of this team came here hoping to find answers to.

I was just 12 years old when I grabbed a shovel from my father's tool collection and began digging a hole in the family backyard. That wasn't just because the thought of digging a hole appealed to me, although that was true, too. It was because I was inspired by fantasies of a long-distant past, along with secret hopes of uncovering lost artifacts from the Native American tribes that once roamed our area—or perhaps even unearth fossils from the dinosaur era. When my mother strolled out hours later and found me at the bottom of a seven-foot hole, she was horrified and ordered me out immediately, fearful that I might suffocate if those damp walls were to collapse on me. Well, she did have a point.

I've often believed that our childhood obsessions harbor the seeds of our later interests and ambitions as adults, and my own fascination with the past and "digging deeper" certainly seemed to foreshadow mine. Among other things, it led to an amateur interest in any and all things related to paleontology, archaeology, and—most of all—Egypt. That curiosity continued well into my later years and led to a series of unusual experiences that I'd eventually have in that extraordinary land. What I'd like to recount here is one such experience that took place in 1997 involving a little-known chamber deep underground on the Giza Plateau, and which has been the source of considerable speculation but also considerable misinformation.

But to do that, we need to start at the beginning.

John Anthony West and Friends

During my time at the Theosophical Society, I came to know an independent researcher named John Anthony West, who published a provocative book titled *Serpent in the Sky: The High Wisdom of Ancient Egypt*. I first read it in the mid-1980s, and was captivated by its ideas, which explored the "symbolist" theory of Egypt first articulated by the writer Schwaller de Lubicz (1887-1961).

In a series of densely written books and essays, de Lubicz suggested that ancient Egypt possessed a far greater degree of wisdom than has generally been acknowledged by contemporary academics, and that was subtly encoded in the symbolism of its monuments, architectural designs, and mythologies. One of my duties working for the Society was that of acquisitions editor, so when I discovered that John's book had gone out of print I called and asked him about our acquiring the rights for a reprint—and so it was that Quest Books released a new and updated version of his book in 1993.

John introduced me to several of the individuals he was working with, in particular a Boston geologist by the name of Robert
Schoch and an old friend of John's named, Boris Said. The three of
them were joining forces (along with director Bill Cote) to produce
a TV special for NBC called *Mystery of the Sphinx*. Initially broadcast
in 1993, it was hosted by actor Charlton Heston and argued that
the Great Sphinx of Egypt might be thousands of years older than
commonly dated, something suggested by unique weathering patterns along its body and the surrounding enclosure. In addition
to doing well in the ratings—it beat out the network premiere of
Dances with Wolves, which *no* one expected—the show went on to
win two Emmys and triggered debates on the pages of academic
journals for years to come. John's star was definitely on the rise,
and mainstream Egyptologists were none too happy about it.

Throughout the entire 1990's I watched from the sidelines as
a fascination for mysterious treasures and ancient civilizations
reached a fevered pitch throughout the culture. But a special interest seemed to spring up around the search for the so-called "Hall
of Records." According to popular legend, this is a repository of lost
knowledge which holds the key to humanity's forgotten past and
which now lies hidden somewhere beneath the sands of Egypt, or
some similarly exotic location. If we are to believe passing references
in Egyptian lore to the lost "Books of Thoth," something roughly
fitting that description may well have existed, but hard evidence has
proven elusive. There were quite a few who believed that a hollow
space detected beneath the Sphinx's paw by West, Schoch, and their
seismologist, Thomas Dobecki, might well hold a key to that mystery.

Though I kept in close touch with West over the coming years,
I also began communicating frequently with his partner Boris. Or
perhaps I should say, John's *ex*-partner, since they had a falling out
over a dispute concerning the profits from the NBC special. As
Hemingway-esque and barrel-chested a character as I've ever met,
Boris lived a life of high adventure that included race car driving

and two stints in the Olympics as the head of a bobsled team, among many other things. John and Boris had known each other since childhood, but things had now taken a very bad turn. Not being privy to the intimate details of their dispute, I can't pass judgment on it one way or another, and will have to leave it for others to make up their own minds about what really happened between them.

It was during one phone conversation with Boris in 1996 that he told me about an intriguing development taking shape in Egypt that he was clearly excited about. It involved an expedition to Cairo that was being organized along with members of the Edgar Cayce foundation, the A.R.E. (Association for Research and Enlightenment), along with a mystically-inclined scientist named Dr. James ("J.J.") Hurtak. The purpose of this upcoming expedition was to explore and film a mysterious chamber roughly 100 feet underground on the Giza Plateau, located several hundred yards behind the Sphinx. Due to high water levels, it had never been fully investigated before, but now that those levels were receding it seemed more accessible.

Boris Said (center)

Boris had known about this spot on the Plateau for several years already, but at the urging of Hurtak, he grew increasingly convinced they would find something important in that chamber deep underground. As a result, Boris enlisted the involvement of the Edgar Cayce group, with the expedition to be bankrolled largely by a wealthy member of that organization, Dr. Joseph Schor. According to Boris, it was set to take place in February of 1997, and to my surprise, he asked if I'd like to come along and observe the proceedings in a journalistic capacity. He'd read and liked *The Waking Dream*, and thought I might be able to bring a different perspective to the expedition. It was an offer I couldn't refuse.

Passage to Egypt
On arriving in Cairo that first night, I made some calls and arranged to meet a few of the other team members near the front entrance of the Mena House, a posh hotel in the grand colonial style just a stone's throw from the pyramids. As night fell across the Plateau, a small van pulled up to the curb with Boris and Hurtak inside, with their wives alongside them. After some cursory introductions, we headed over to the Great Pyramid where we found others from the team waiting for us. The gathering on this first night was intended to inaugurate the expedition on an auspicious note.

The sense of anticipation amongst all the team members was electric. I had studied the astrology of this period beforehand, so I was keenly aware of the epic conjunction of Jupiter and Uranus that was taking place that very night. That timing seemed almost too extraordinary to be strictly by accident, and led me to wonder whether Dr. Schor hadn't arranged this expedition on the advice of an astrologer (which he probably did).

We carefully made our way in through the pyramid's entrance and up the long "Grand Gallery," and finally into the King's Chamber. Once we all settled into our spots against the outer walls, Hurtak then led the group through a three-hour spoken ceremony, with his voice and language taking on near-Biblical inflections at times. The litany of topics he covered included the seventy-six names of the Pharaohs, the Nile journey as a symbolic voyage of the soul, an invocation of blessings from the disembodied Pharaohs, the significance of the three stars in the belt of Orion, and the unique sonic properties of this room. There was more: he alluded to the Hall of Records, the importance of the missing pyramid capstone, and the Kabbalistic relationship between the four-lettered name of God and the four corners of the pyramid's base. James casts a very wide net, that was obvious.

With that portion of the ceremony finished, each team member took turns lying inside the sarcophagus for a few moments, while Hurtak and I helped them climb into and out of it safely. By the time the formal ceremony was over, most of the team members were exhausted, some of that due simply to jet lag from the long flight over, while a few others seemed deeply moved by Hurtak's ceremony. Glancing at Boris, I saw tears running down his cheeks, and asked what he was feeling. He said Hurtak's ceremony touched a deep chord for him, though he couldn't articulate why. I found it fascinating, too, but was grappling with such intense back pain from the hard surfaces we'd been sitting on for three hours that I looked forward to returning to my motel and the comfort of a soft bed.

Old and New
Early the next morning, the investigation began in earnest. "Well, here goes nothing," Boris quipped as we set out before dawn toward the Plateau in his van. The early morning skies around the Plateau exude a quality of clarity and peace quite unlike anything I've experienced anywhere else. The guards waved our vehicle past the checkpoint leading to the pyramids, as we drove carefully

towards the site where we'd establish our base of operations for the day.

Members of the film crew hauled their elaborate equipment down the steep metal ladder in the well-shaft, while the rest of us milled around up top, trying our best to find shade as the temperature soared to 100 degrees F. The conversations amongst the team members pivoted around the pressing questions of the day. Was the chamber below simply a natural cavity, as some believed? Or was it an ancient ceremonial room that fell into disrepair? Or might it even be an "anteroom" which connected to another, even more important chamber—an ancient library, perhaps? More than one team member was hoping for that possibility.

At one point during the afternoon well-known Egyptologist Mark Lehner came by to check out our group. I had met him once before, at a scientific conference in Chicago put on in 1992 by the American Association for the Advancement of Science, where he and Robert Schoch debated the true age of the Sphinx. Throughout this entire period, Lehner was probably the most prominent critic of West and Schoch's theories about the Sphinx, and he'd obviously gotten word of our group's presence on the Plateau that day. Nodding towards the entrance of the shaft, he remarked to a couple of us standing around, in a teasing way, "So...have you found the Hall of Records down there yet?"

There was no small irony for me in that comment. Just one year earlier I'd been looking through the Theosophical library and came across a thin volume titled *Egyptian Heritage*, which was a sympathetic treatment of Edgar Cayce's writings on Atlantis, Egypt, and the Hall of Records. The author of the book? None other than Mark Lehner—the self-professed skeptic of all fringe theories associated with Egypt. He had apparently started out an avid student of Cayce's theories, but during the course of his academic studies underwent a conversion to a more conservative and evidence-based view of ancient Egypt. Or that's how it appeared in public, anyway. Who knows what he really believed in private.

Because of that past affiliation with the Edgar Cayce foundation, Mark remained friends with Joseph Schor and his colleague Joe Jahoda through the years. After he walked away from our group, I heard Jahoda say that Mark actually climbed down to the bottom of the well-shaft as early as the 1970s, and suspected even then it might hold some real importance. Why, I wondered? "Because of its proximity to the pyramids," Jahoda explained. "That implied to Mark it must have been exceedingly important to the ancient Egyptians. But the water table was too high back then for him or anyone else to do any real investigation of it."

That first day was a long one, extending well past sunset, as Boris and some of the others lumbered back up the ladder beneath the cobalt sky. As I helped him carry some of his gear back to the van parked several yards away, I was taken aback by the startling sight of green laser beams darting across the plateau all around us, creating stunning designs along the ground as well as the face of the pyramid. I immediately realized it was a sound-and-light show being staged further down the Plateau for tourists. It made for an anachronistic blend of past and future, with ancient history coming up against space-age technology. Yet strangely enough, it all seemed perfectly appropriate.

The Discovery
It was sometime during the course of February 18th that the expedition's cameraman, Garrett, made the initial find. He was down in the chamber positioning the tripod for his movie camera when

he suddenly realized he was standing on a stone slab of some sort. Clearing away the dirt, it became obvious this wasn't any ordinary rock, since it looked too smooth, too polished. Word quickly percolated back up to the crew members on top, and before long rumors began circulating as to what this might be.

Later that day while everyone was away on break, I climbed down the rusty metal ladder bolted into the sides of the narrow shaft to see what was down there for myself. The entire length of the shaft is staggered into three distinct levels. The first level opens out into a relatively small space littered with debris; next, the shaft plummeted down a sheer vertical drop of about 70 feet, and the old metal ladder I was using felt precarious at points. But the descent was exhilarating, too, since I felt as though each step down was taking me closer to the heart of an ancient mystery. For a split second, my mind recalled those feelings I had as a child digging that hole in my parent's backyard, looking for remnants of a lost past.

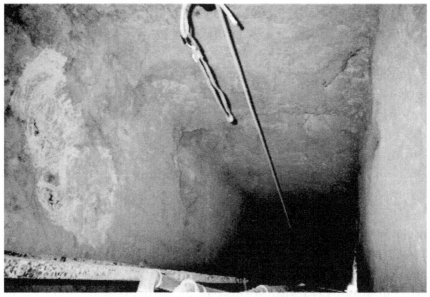

Looking down the shaft towards the "Tomb of Osiris."

On that second level down, I encountered a chamber with seven niches or "cubicles" carved into the rock walls, two of which contained large sarcophagi made of heavy stone. One of those was solid black and surprisingly smooth, almost like it had been constructed using modern engineering tools; the other one looked much rougher and grayish in color. They were large, and I learned each one weighed over 20 tons. It boggled my mind trying to imagine how the ancients could have moved these massive sarcophagi into this underground chamber, especially considering there are no signs of damage on the walls of the narrow shaft at all. Fascinating as all that was, though, I was anxious to see what was further down the shaft, so I carefully made my way down the ladder to the very bottom of a 30-foot drop.

At first glance, that lowest room looked like a rectangular cavern, but in very rough shape. I was struck by the sense of profound antiquity which permeated this space. Some of that was obviously due to the fact that, unlike so many popular tourist sites in this country, this one was completely unrestored. The air in the chamber was thick and musty, almost suffocating. There was something slightly spooky about it as well, not just because of its ruinous state but the sight of a few human bones protruding from the muddy water along its edges. That was unsettling in a way, as if I'd intruded into someone's final resting place. I couldn't help but wonder if there might be something to those legends about curses against trespassers to these ancient sites, so to play it safe I offered up a few silent protective prayers before venturing in further.

I could see that the chamber was completely flooded along its outer rim on three sides, and that I was standing on a kind of island extending out from the shaft's entrance. At the far end of this "island" I noticed the broken remains of two large pillars, both of them square and truncated. To me, the room had more the feel of an archaic temple than a conventional crypt.

A rough sketch of the chamber I did during one of my visits inside. The partially exposed stone slab is to the left, the central "pool" of water is in the middle (flanked by two truncated pillars to the right), and a watery moat surrounding the island on three sides. On the far right is the mysterious upper corner cavity which suggested a possible passage beyond the chamber (which has yet to be determined).

And there, right before me, amidst the rocks and the mud, I could see the smooth stone surface the others spoke about, roughly one square foot in size and just a few yards from the entrance into the chamber. It wasn't obvious whether or not this was man-made, but to my untrained eye it seemed far too smooth to be natural, and hinted at something larger underneath.

Theories above were rampant amongst team members as to what this might be. Some suspected it was the surface of a sarcophagus, while a few others thought it could indicate a passageway to yet another chamber—perhaps even the legendary Hall of Records itself? Unfortunately, the team only had a filming permit, not an archeological one, so we weren't allowed to disturb anything in the chamber. Just to make sure our curiosity didn't get the better of us, the Egyptians posted an observer to accompany us the entire time, who watched every move we made. Considering how much thievery and damage takes place at many of these sites, that was understandable. But it was frustrating, too, since we knew that removing even a small amount of dirt from around that slab might reveal what it was, or what lay beneath it.

This was all about to change, however.

The next day while I was down in the chamber with Boris, Hurtak, and a couple members of the film crew, the Egyptian who had been assigned to watch us climbed back up the ladder to take a short bathroom break. Those of us standing around all looked at each other as if reading one another's minds—as we then piled onto the ground to quickly (and carefully) use our fingers to scrape away as much dirt from around the stone slab as possible. We knew full well this was outside of official protocol, but we also realized this was a once-in-a-lifetime opportunity, and were determined not to damage anything in the process. Over the next few minutes it quickly became apparent that this stone slab must have been carved by human hands, and wasn't simply a natural feature. We were excited, but also mystified. What were we looking at, exactly?

Word about the exposed slab spread quickly amongst the team members above, and the team's technical expert, Thomas Dobecki, and his two helpers hauled their ground-penetrating radar equipment down into the chamber the next day for a closer look. Scanning the dirt floor of the chamber with his equipment, he detected what appeared to be a hollow space just beneath the slab. He said the stone itself seemed to be roughly thirty inches thick, and beneath that appeared to be a possible tunnel descending in an easterly direction towards the Sphinx. That ignited everyone's imagination further, since it might indicate a passageway, a hidden chamber, or at the very least, a previously unknown sarcophagus. Boris in particular was banking on the possibility of a secret passageway possibly extending from this room. Whatever it was, anticipation was reaching a fever pitch amongst the team members as to what might be next.

The Tide Turns

When Egyptian officials caught wind of what we'd uncovered down below, the entire mood of the expedition changed. I now saw local officials whispering to one another off to the sides, obviously trying to figure out what to do about this unexpected turn of events. Boris and Joseph Schor tried to play down what we'd found while talking with Plateau officials, and began negotiating with them over just how much more research or filming would be allowed from that point on. Boris in particular was anxious to obtain permission for exploring the underground chamber further—especially beneath the mysterious stone slab. But Boris and Joseph now seem blocked at every turn, with the rest of the group now growing restless. It was clear to me the officials in charge suspected this could be something important, and didn't want to lose control of the situation.

It was a couple of mornings after the initial discovery that I arrived on site to find the film crew busy setting up for an interview with Zahi Hawass, which was planned to take place directly in front of the Sphinx. Several minutes later Hawass himself arrived on the scene. Next to the president of Egypt, Zahi was probably the most well-known figure in Egypt. He could be a world-class ham, too. For years if you turned on any TV show about Egypt you invariably saw Zahi's face front and center. I always had the feeling Zahi could sniff a camera from a mile away, maybe 1000 miles away. It was well-known that his ambitious streak made him more than a few enemies over the years, both inside and out of Egypt. Boris seemed to drift in and out of that category himself over the years, wavering between warm friendship and ice-cold animosity towards the man. [1]

Yet every time I began to feel like Zahi might be too self-serving for his own good, I'd hear some story which portrayed him more favorably. Like the story my friend Rosemary Clark told me about the first time she traveled to Egypt and approached Zahi about spending a night inside the Great Pyramid—this, long before it was the fashionable thing to do amongst New Age seekers. Impressed by her sincerity, he immediately arranged for her to spend the night there alone, undisturbed by guards or other visitors. When she offered to pay him for his help, he steadfastly refused. As anyone familiar with Egypt knows, finding an official in this country who refused money is a rare thing indeed, and suggested to me there may be something more spiritual lurking beneath all that bluster and bombast. Maybe.

I was curious to know more about the man. Like Mark Lehner, Zahi was a vocal critic of all "fringe" theories about the Giza Plateau and its pyramids; his famously derisive term for proponents of such theories was *pyramidiots*. Yet surprisingly, he started out—like Lehner—as an avid student of Edgar Cayce's writings. When I saw Joe Jahoda standing off to the side waiting for their interview to start, I asked him for his honest opinion of the man, since they'd been friends for decades by that point. Joe proceeded to tell me how he and his colleagues at the A.R.E. helped put Zahi through college back at the University of Pennsylvania years earlier. He spoke with obvious affection for Zahi, citing the difficulties he faced in

America as a foreign student on his arrival. "People don't realize how tough it was for him when he came to America. He barely spoke any English at all, yet he managed to make his way through school."

Beneath the Pyramid

Over the next few days negotiations with the local officials dragged on, so Boris decided to use his extra time to finish up some other projects. One of those involved taking the film crew over to shoot some extraneous scenes in the King's Chamber inside the Great Pyramid. But as commonly happens with film projects, this one proceeded at a snail's pace, so I took the opportunity to explore other parts of the pyramid on my own.

The Great Pyramid is an engineering marvel, but also a great mystery. Aside from the lingering question as to how it was built, there is the problem of *when* it was built. In the 1980s a researcher from the University of Washington, Robert Wenke, carbon-dated samples of mortar obtained from the pyramid which contained wood, charcoal and reed, and yielded the surprising result that it was several hundred years older than previously believed. Later tests conducted by Robert Temple, using a different method, corroborated those results (we'll come back to that later). Findings like these are perplexing since they seem to place the construction of the Great Pyramid near the very dawn of Egyptian civilization, long before it's generally believed Egyptians had either the knowledge or social organization to accomplish such a feat.

After carefully examining the so-called "Grand Gallery" which cuts at an angle up through the pyramid, I decided to search out the subterranean pit beneath its foundation, which is accessible via a narrow, slanted passageway extending down into the ground several hundred feet. Carved out of the plateau's limestone bedrock, its narrow size forces visitors to make their way in a crouched-down position for the length of its two-hundred feet. This structure is no playground for claustrophobics, rest assured. That downward passageway raises questions of its own regarding the building of the Great Pyramid, and how long it actually took to create. As independent researcher Gordon White summed it up,

Constraint analysis is an engineering technique to determine where the bottlenecks lie in a building project. That is, which steps in a construction cannot be made to go faster and/ or also hold up the rest of the project...With specific reference to the Great Pyramid, the descending passage...is only 42 inches square, meaning that only one worker at any one time could be carving it out. This provides a neat and measurable example of constraint analysis: it would have taken almost twice Khufu's reign for a single person to carve out this passageway using a dolerite pounder, and that is working twenty-four hours a day. Not only is the pyramid too old to be a tomb, its construction cannot fit into the twenty-something year reign of Khufu." [2]

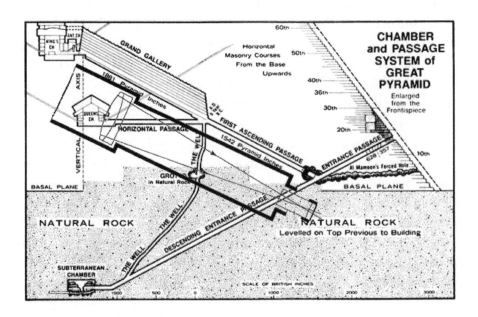

I finally emerged into the pit at the shaft's bottom, which appears far more rough-hewn than the rest of the Pyramid. Its original function still isn't fully understood. While some believe it's an abandoned burial chamber, others suggest it may have served ceremonial or ritualistic purposes, but the simple fact of the matter is, we don't know.

Standing in the silence of the underground chamber, something about its muffled acoustics caught my attention, so on a hunch I decided to stomp down on the dirt floor as hard as I could. To my surprise, the resonance from that sound seemed to reverberate all the way up through the Pyramid, as if the entire monument had become a gigantic gong. When I mentioned that phenomenon down in the pit to John Anthony West several months later, he was surprised, since he'd never heard anything about it before. It reminded me of another experience I had in the Great Pyramid during a tour with John back in 1994. While lying in the sarcophagus and chanting a few obligatory "Oms" with John's group that day—practically a rite of passage for many of those visiting the Great Pyramid—at one point I hit a certain note that caused the sarcophagus around me to resonate in an uncanny way, and my entire body to vibrate.

Between that sound up in the King's Chamber and this one down inside the pit, it was easy to believe sonic effects like these were intentionally designed to be part of this structure's function. The more time I've spent inside the Great Pyramid, the more I can't help thinking this extraordinary structure might represent an advanced magical technology the likes of which we can't fully comprehend, possibly involving a complex network of intentions, correspondences, and God-knows-what subtle energies, all coalescing to impact—what? The consciousness of humans inside of it? The broader life and destiny of Egypt? Perhaps even the entire world? I don't claim to know, but I have no doubt there is far more to this structure than meets the eye.

The underground "pit" deep beneath the Great Pyramid

After climbing back up from the pit through the passageway, I walked back outside of the pyramid and found a ledge slightly higher up on one of its sides, where I sat beneath the stars and watched the lights of Cairo sparkling across the horizon

The Rogue Scientist

The next day I made a point of spending some time speaking with Dr. Hurtak. We'd been conversing in short bursts over the previous few days but never for long. I'd known about his work before coming on this trip, chiefly in connection with a book he'd written in 1973 titled *Forbidden Knowledge: Keys of Enoch*. It was a mysterious but hefty volume that somehow managed to sell over 100,000 copies without any advertising, which is no small feat. The book struck me as an unusual blend of scientific knowledge and quasi-Biblical phrasing, an admixture of styles that mirrored his own background as a scientist who supposedly underwent a spiritual transformation. I knew there was some controversy surrounding him, some of it explicitly conspiratorial in nature (see the book *Stargate Conspiracy* to learn more about that). Personally, though, I found him to be an intelligent and sensitive fellow. I'd heard some unusual stories about him myself over the years, and during our conversations he alluded to the mystical experience he had back in the 70s. The fact that he was a scientist with over a hundred research papers to his name suggested he was a serious thinker, but the sheer strangeness of some of those tales made it hard for me to know just *what* to think. One day I came out and asked Boris for his opinion of those stories.

Boris Said (left), Dr. J.J. Hurtak (right)

"You know, I don't know what to make of them, Ray, but I gotta say, I've seen some pretty strange things around him myself."

"Like what?"

"Well, take the time I was sitting in a room with James as he read aloud from a research paper he'd just written. It began to get dark in the room, yet James continued reading from his paper. That seemed odd at first, because now it was getting very hard to see. That's when I noticed it: there were beams of light emanating from his eyes down to the page. I swear to God, Ray. I saw this with my own eyes. I couldn't believe it, but there it was. I didn't say anything about it to James at the time, but later on I mentioned it to (James' wife) Desireé, and she said, 'So you *saw* that?'—as if she were fully aware of the phenomenon but surprised to hear someone else noticed it, too. She then told me a little bit about the experience he had back in the 70s, and claimed she actually managed to capture some of the light-phenomena around him on film, which include a faint glow around his body at one point.

"So in answer to your question Ray, I just don't know. But I've seen too much to simply dismiss it all. Besides, he's been right time after time about things that later turned out to be true, and I can't ignore that."

The Archaeology of Souls

I used much of my free time to explore the entire plateau, since my involvement with the team gave me unfettered access to most of the area, often with virtually no one else around. That made for an extraordinary opportunity, and I didn't want to waste it. As with other sacred sites around the world, there is a dramatically different ambience once the hordes of chattering tourists clear out and the mood downshifts into one of deep silence. At dusk, especially, an atmosphere of timeless mystery descends across the Giza Plateau like a golden blanket.

Late one afternoon, while the other team members were off pursuing their own projects, I set out to explore the maze of ancient ruins and tombs carved out of rock just south of the plateau. The sun had set just minutes earlier, creating a dusky glow across the plateau. I was completely alone as I meandered through the man-made pathways and gullies carved into those corridors of stone.

The light grew soft and the environment became quiet, with the maze of ruinous pathways revealing ever more imposing sights at every turn. Finding myself in an area as ancient and sacred as this, where so many thousands lived, worshipped, and died over the millennia, was profoundly humbling, almost ego-shattering. I continued exploring the area for over an hour, feeling at times almost like I was under the influence of a psychedelic drug, even though I wasn't.

I eventually headed back in the direction of the well-shaft, where I saw Hurtak sitting in the group's rented van on the causeway finishing up some paperwork. As I approached him, he seemed curious as to what I'd just experienced, since he saw me from a distance during part of my walk.

"So, Ray, what was happening for you there for you?"

"Just soaking this all in. It's remarkable here. Why do you ask?"

"I had the feeling you were experiencing something unusual. It almost looked like you were half in and out of your body."

It was odd hearing him describe it like that, since that's exactly how it felt—a sense of physical dislocation, almost an out-of-body experience.

Lying in bed later that night reflecting on my experience, I had the vague sense that the energies of all those who lived and died in this area had somehow seeped into my bones, and were a part of me now. I wrote in my journal: "I was surrounded by death on every side, yet I'd never felt quite so alive as I did today."

Aftermath

The next day I called back home to the States and discovered there were urgent matters I needed to take care of, so I would have to return home sooner than expected. But negotiations with Zahi and company had reached a standstill so it didn't much matter whether I departed sooner or later. As it turned out, the expedition drew to a close without any firm conclusions. No treasures or lost civilizations would be uncovered this time around, sadly.

It was roughly one month later that I began noticing rumors on the Internet about the expedition and its supposed discoveries. The speculations were all sensationalistic, ranging from talk about the Hall of Records to alien spaceships uncovered beneath the Plateau. The fact that no hard information about the expedition had been released to the public only fanned the speculative flames further. It was around that time the Boris went on the air to talk with popular radio show host Art Bell about the expedition, spilling the beans before millions of listeners about what had taken place that February—in the process invoking the ire of certain A.R.E. members who had expected him to keep the team's findings confidential for the time being.

Exactly one year later, on February 16th of 1998, I opened a Chicago newspaper to see a story published by the Reuters news service, with the headline: "Egyptians Find Tomb of Ancient God Osiris." It read: "Sinking water levels have revealed a granite sarcophagus of the ancient Egyptian god Osiris in a 30-metre (98 feet) deep tomb at the Giza pyramids, Egyptian archeologist Zahi Hawass said on Wednesday." Apparently, during the twelve months since our team left Cairo, Zahi and his crew had been busy clearing out the chamber, and discovered that the slab we uncovered was indeed the lid to a stone sarcophagus, or royal coffin. It turned out to be empty, and was partially underwater.

Zahi seemed to feel the chamber and its contents weren't really that old, by Egyptian standards, perhaps dating from the period around 600 BCE, give or take 50 to 75 years. He also suggested the archaic chamber could be the mythical "Tomb of Osiris," described in tradition as a stone sarcophagus on an island surrounded by water, deep underground, where Osiris rose from the dead. Could the chamber we explored be that very spot? According to the press releases, Zahi certainly thought so. He went on to declare this was the most important archeological discovery of his entire career. "I never excavated this shaft before because it was always full of water," Zahi said, "but when the water went down about a year ago, we started the adventure."

The most important discovery of *his* career? That took me by surprise, since he made no mention at all of Hurtak, Boris, or the A.R.E., even though they were the ones ultimately responsible for it. I probably shouldn't have been surprised, since Zahi had something of a reputation as a claim-jumper on discoveries set into motion by others. As someone once explained to me, the politics of Egyptology can be as bad as anything you'd find in the halls of Washington, DC.

It was one year later, in March of 1999, that Zahi's work down in the chamber was given worldwide TV exposure in the form of a Fox television special titled *Opening the Lost Tomb, Live!*, hosted by Maury Povich. During the prime-time special, viewers were treated to video footage of the chamber itself, images of the half-submerged sarcophagus and its suspended lid, and of course, Zahi himself presiding proudly over the discovery. It was fascinating to see how the chamber looked now with much of the mud and debris cleared out, and the sarcophagus revealed more fully now. But it was disappointing too, seeing how Boris, Hurtak, and the A.R.E. team were essentially erased from the history books.

To his credit, though, Boris never let that theft of credit bother him, since he had other projects to pursue, including a TV special that hoped to finally explore the suspected chamber beneath the Sphinx's paw. Both Boris and Joseph Schor were eager to procure financial backing for the project, but knew that wouldn't be easy. In addition to all the baseline expenses involved, there were the large sums of money needed to "reimburse" all the Egyptian officials involved. However they budgeted it, it wouldn't be a cheap project. At one point Boris and Joseph even arranged a meeting with media mogul Rupert Murdoch in his London offices, since he had shown interest in the project. When I asked Boris why Murdoch of all people would want to get involved in something like that, Boris simply answered, "Well, Murdoch is a Mason."

They eventually had their meeting with Rupert, though nothing ever came of it. Boris had other projects, including ones in Japan, Africa, and Central America, most of them in collaboration with Hurtak. But he returned to the Giza Plateau several more times to do further research into the unique acoustics of the Great

Pyramid. After returning from one of those trips, he claimed that
what he had uncovered there would dwarf any other discoveries in
Egypt, even including the long-sought-for Hall of Records.

He was hesitant to reveal exactly what they found until all the
results were analyzed, except to say that one of them involved
strange, wave-like hollows they detected beneath the floor of the
King's Chamber. "That's probably what's responsible for the room's
unique acoustics," he suggested. He said that a professor from the
University of Washington was currently in the process of convert-
ing their mountains of data into computer simulations, and they
were supposedly a revelation to behold.

Sadly, that's the last I ever heard of those findings. Along with
a series of legal problems, Boris's health deteriorated, and when he
was finally diagnosed with a cancerous lump on his liver he stub-
bornly resisted chemotherapy. "If I go," he said, "I want to go while
riding down the Amazon River taking ayahuasca."

During our next few phone calls he sounded increasingly weary
and short of breath. In March of 2002, I called to finish up a conversation we'd begun several days earlier about a project we hoped to do
involving research being done by my friend Barbara Keller. Boris's
long-time friend Beth Melnick answered the phone, and when I asked
to speak with him, there was a long pause. She solemnly informed
me that Boris had died just the day before. He hadn't checked
out while riding down the Amazon ingesting ayahuasca after all;
he passed away quietly shortly after watching the latest broadcast of
the Academy Awards. Which is just as well, I suppose, since he always
had fun watching the ceremony, so at least went out doing something
he enjoyed.

I knew they hadn't spoken to each other in years, so I decided
to call up John Anthony West that afternoon to give him the news.
He was as taken aback by it as I had been. As with Joseph Campbell,
it's surprising when a figure like Boris passes away, since he not
only seemed larger-than-life but maybe even larger-than-death.
But any sadness John felt about Boris was clearly tempered by that

longstanding feud which tore them apart years earlier, and several days later he posted the following words on the Internet:

> Those who met Boris at any time over the course of his 69 years, even briefly, probably will not have forgotten him; physically powerful, radiating an almost superhuman, high octane intensity, with a quick, coarse humor and an even quicker, coarser temper, infinitely resourceful especially when his back was to the wall — which it usually was, since he found ways to make sure that's where it stayed.

Decoding the Tomb of Osiris: What Does it Mean?

As the years went on, I heard little else about the Tomb of Osiris, other than more fantastical speculations circulating on the Internet. Those included suggestions that it's actually an interdimensional portal which can only be opened by someone with the appropriate DNA. Well, okay.

But in 2016 my interest was sparked anew by research I came across by independent researcher Robert Temple. Temple first gained attention in the 1970s for a controversial book titled *The Sirius Mystery*, suggesting a possible connection between the Dogon tribe further south in Africa and the ancient Egyptian civilization up north. But in a more recent book, *Egyptian Dawn*, Temple focused heavily on the Giza Plateau itself, and devoted an entire chapter to the Osiris shaft. [3] (What follows may seem somewhat academic or technical to some, but I encourage you to take your time digesting these points, as the implications are both fascinating and far-reaching.)

Addressing the different levels of the shaft, Temple suggested it was likely constructed in stages during different historical periods. [2] While the conventional wisdom suggested that it dates back to the so-called "Saitic" period, which extended from 664 BC to 525 BC (relatively recent in Egyptian history, in other words), Temple challenged that view and claimed that it was considerably older. How did he come to that conclusion? That's where things start to get interesting.

I'm standing here alongside one of two remaining sarcophagi on the
second level of the shaft.

As mentioned earlier, the second level of the Osiris shaft contains two large stone sarcophagi. Temple found that the black one with the smooth surface was made of granite, a commonly-used stone throughout ancient Egypt and relatively obtainable for creating ancient tombs and monuments. However, he discovered that the second, more roughly-hewn sarcophagus on that same level was carved from a more obscure stone called dacite.

How obscure? Aside from the fact it apparently wasn't used at any other time in ancient Egypt for creating monuments, statues, or sarcophagi, there doesn't appear to be a vein of dacite anywhere in Africa large enough to produce a sarcophagus like the one on that second level of the Osiris shaft. To the best of anyone's knowledge, the dacite deposits closest to Cairo are hundreds of miles away.

Think about that for a second. This means the Egyptians would have had to transport this massively heavy object across great distances overland, before lowering it down into this relatively narrow shaft. How they managed to do all that is enough of a mystery, especially considering the dimensions of the shaft; but *why* they did so is just as much of one, especially when you consider how much easier it would have been to simply use far more accessible Aswan granite. If nothing else, it points to the enormous importance the ancient Egyptians placed on different types of stone and their symbolic meanings.

But that's not the only mystery. One of Temple's projects involved attempting to date the monuments and objects of the Giza Plateau using a method invented by nuclear physicist Ioannis Liritzis called 'optical thermoluminescence.' No instruments can carbon date solid stone, of course, but thermoluminescence can roughly determine a stone's *last exposure to sunlight*, which can indirectly help to determine a general time frame. Using that method, Temple dated the construction of the dacite sarcophagus on the second level to roughly 2800 BC, give or take 550 years either way—providing us with a window ranging roughly anywhere from

3350 BC to 2200 BC. That raises the intriguing possibility that the dacite sarcophagus could be several centuries older than the Giza pyramids themselves, as conventionally dated. If so, that would make the dacite sarcophagus one of the oldest objects on the Giza Plateau.

But what about the third level down in the shaft, and the granite sarcophagus in the so-called "Tomb of Osiris" that our group examined? When Temple applied the thermoluminescence method to it, he found it was somewhat younger in age—although still much older than Zahi's estimate. It dated back to about 1700 BC, give or take 400 years. That gave it a comfortable range of having been constructed somewhere between 2370 BC to 1270 BC., roughly during the Middle Kingdom.

While that means there may be some overlap between the ages of the second and third levels of the shaft, it does suggest that the second level is older than the third (which isn't surprising, actually, since in the process of digging down, workers would have reached the second level before reaching the third)—which places the second level in the time frame of the "Old Kingdom" era, if not even earlier.

As a result, Robert Temple concluded that while the second level was originally created as a tomb for important figures, perhaps including an early Pharaoh, the third level at the very bottom of the shaft was probably created later for more ritualistic purposes. To say it all a little differently, the second level may be more significant for archaeological reasons, due to its great age, while the third level may be more important for symbolic and ritualistic reasons.

But what did those rituals within the "Tomb of Osiris" on that lowest level consist of, exactly? Inspired partly by the work of Egyptologist Rosalie David, Temple offers up some intriguing guesses as to what these may have looked like. At another site in Egypt called Abydos, there are the remains of a sunken temple commonly referred to as the "Osireion," which was also believed to commemorate the burial and resurrection of Osiris. By studying the rituals practiced there, as described in inscriptions found both in the Osireion and the adjoining Temple of Osiris, he suggests we can plausibly reconstruct some of what may have transpired in that chamber down in the Giza well-shaft as well. Like the Osireion, *it's possible that the Tomb of Osiris served as a secret place of initiation and ritual re-enactment of the death by drowning, burial and resurrection of Osiris.*

Temple speculates this ceremony could have taken the form of the empty sarcophagus being opened, the priest or Pharaoh lying in the container, then having the lid placed over them. This may have even included the act of "drowning" in the sarcophagus, with the participant either using an air tube to breathe or drawing on the remaining air supply within the container. Shortly afterwards, when the theorized ceremony calling Osiris to rise from the dead took place, complete with singing and praying, the lid could have been removed and the "resurrected" figure rose up to be "born again." The ceremony may have been attended by a priestess representing Isis who was presiding over the ritual resurrection. As such, the empty sarcophagus in level three could be seen as a symbolic statement in much the same way that the empty tomb of Jesus was seen by his followers as a statement about his resurrection, and of life everlasting.

While this is all speculative, I find it compelling, certainly more than any other theory concerning the chamber I've come across. In the end, Temple sums things up this way:

> In conclusion, I should say that the Osiris Shaft can never now be relegated to the status of a secondary feature of the Giza Plateau on the assumption that it is a Saitic burial shaft dating from the period 664 BC- 525 BC. This is now seen to be definitely not the case. The bottom level of the shaft is probably Middle Kingdom, and Level Two is probably no later than the Fourth Dynasty. And what is more, [the dacite sarcophagus in level two], being made of a unique stone that occurs nowhere else—to our knowledge—amongst the surviving remains of the ancient Egyptian civilization, and

being so unexpectedly ancient in date, must now be seen as one of the oldest and most precious of all carved objects to survive in the whole of Egypt. *Also, the 'Tomb of Osiris' must now be viewed as being of extraordinary importance, whether as a mystical burial site, or more likely as a mystical religious site for initiations or ceremonies connected with the Osirian religion during the second millennium BC.* (Emphasis mine.) [4]

A multitude of questions remain about the site and its contents. For instance, some continue to wonder whether there is a tunnel or channel leading out of the chamber apart from the main shaft our group entered it through. While we were down in the chamber, for instance, we clearly saw a small cavity off in the northwest corner of the room which appeared to be hacked out of the wall and seemed to lead out beyond the chamber. (See my earlier drawing of the chamber, specifically the spot near the question mark.) As of this writing, the latest reports claim that Zahi's crew sent a remote-controlled robot through that opening and found that a small channel extended about 150 feet before an accumulation of mud prevented any further exploration. [5]

Another intriguing clue lies in the fact that the water in the moat around the central "island" where the sarcophagus lies seems to be fed by a natural source. Unlike more polluted water sources further down the Giza Plateau, this water even seems drinkable, and was supposedly used for years as a source of well water for locals. If so, what is the source of the water? As Temple points out, the rock walls and floor of the chamber seem too solid for there to be random leaks. So does it enter through an artificial channel deliberately constructed by the ancients? Apart from the mind-boggling logistical and engineering challenges that would have posed, it also raises the possibility there may still be an opening located underwater somewhere in that room. Clearly, there is still work yet to be done to unlock the full significance of the Tomb of Osiris, not to mention the Giza Plateau generally. [6]

Some Final Thoughts

Reflecting back on this distant culture, it can sometimes feel like one is looking at an alien civilization, its customs and rituals being so far removed from our own. Yet despite those differences, there are elements that feel strangely familiar to us in other ways.

Consider those theorized rituals which may have occurred in that chamber deep underground involving the ceremonial death and resurrection of Osiris. Not long after reading Temple's book and his speculations about the chamber, I was invited to watch a friend perform in an Easter pageant being put on by a mega-church in my area. As I watched the actors on stage recreating the death of Christ and his resurrection, complete with a depiction of the stone being rolled away from the tomb, as well as Christ's radiant ascension into heaven (all portrayed with very clever lighting and stage effects), I couldn't help notice the similarities to what might have unfolded in that archaic chamber deep in the Plateau. Despite the superficial differences, it's clear that our present-day civilization continues to celebrate the death and resurrection of a divine being in ways that echo practices of ancient times.

Or consider the simple but ubiquitous Christian practice of baptism itself, in which a person is lowered into water and symbolically "reborn" into a new spiritual life. Looked at with fresh eyes, this ritual shares an obvious resonance with those in which an initiate or Pharaoh in Egypt may have been immersed in water and "reborn" into a new life. Even without the added element of water, some have suggested that the sarcophagus in the King's Chamber in the Great Pyramid served a kindred function, of facilitating the symbolic deaths and rebirths of initiates, priests, even Pharaohs. It's also worth noting that modern Masonic ceremonies feature their own death/rebirth ritual that initiates must undergo to be admitted into their order.

Whether these varied rites of death and resurrection in our own time were handed down over the millennia through some unbroken line of transmission, or simply reflect a perennial archetype that recurs throughout all time and space, it does suggest that our spiritual impulses may not be quite so different from those of our forebears as we'd like to believe. *Plus les choses changent…*

A Christian Artist's Conception of Resurrection

Postscript: John Anthony West passed away on February 6, 2018, at age 85, from a case of rapidly developing cancer. Until just a few months prior to his death, he had been leading trips to Egypt, and in our last telephone conversation remarked, "I'll know it's time for me to quit leading tours when I can no longer climb up to the top of the Great Pyramid." Little did either of us suspect during that conversation he wouldn't be climbing any more pyramids—not in this world, anyway. Rest in peace, John.

This article first appeared, in abbreviated form, in the anthology Darklore: Vol. 10 *(editor: Greg Taylor), 2019.*

CHAPTER 14

THE THINNING VEIL

Whereas my time in Egypt felt in some ways like wandering through a dream, returning to Illinois felt more like waking up from one. My marriage to Judith had reached a turning point, and after struggling for ten years to make things work between us, which included dealing with the loss of a baby, we divorced but remained good friends. Things were coming to a head for me at the Theosophical Society as well, in part due to disagreements I was having with certain members of the administration.

It was at that point I began thinking of leaving my job there, especially so as to have more time to work on my second book, *The Dawn of Aquarius*, concerning the doctrine of the Great Ages. I had been offered long-distance work as associate editor for The Mountain Astrologer magazine in California, and hoped that, combined with earnings from my horoscope readings, that would be enough to tide me over and allow me time for writing. I moved into an apartment in downtown Wheaton, left the Theosophical Society, and during that first year sank my heart and soul into finishing the book.

As it turned out, my income wasn't enough to pay the bills and I wound up taking a part-time job as a hypnotist at a weight loss clinic in nearby Naperville. Hypnosis was one of the skills I studied while I was in my 20s desperately trying to find my footing in one livelihood or another. While the hypnosis practice never quite got off the ground back then, it was turning out to be a valuable skill now. I enjoyed working with the clients who came through the center, several thousand of them in all, and it gave me the chance to work on my writing the other days of the week. As a result, in 2002 my second book finally came out, with a new title, changed by the publisher to *Signs of the Times*. (Non-writers are often surprised to hear writers often have little control over the title of their books, that being one of the trade-offs of working with a publisher.)

Then, several years later, everything changed in the blink of an eye.

Caretaking

My parents had been living since the 1980s on the east coast of Florida, in the great but decidedly sketchy little town of Cocoa Beach, not far from the rocket launch pads over at Cape Canaveral. My father had passed away in 1996, and ten years later my mother went blind as a result of a medical mistake. She'd been heavily involved with art since retirement, and was planning a series of paintings for the coming years, so the loss of her eyesight was especially heartbreaking for her. She fell into a deep depression, and after seven years at the hypnosis clinic, I quit my job in 2007 to move down there and take care of her during those final years.

I knew beforehand it would be difficult, but had little idea just how difficult that would turn out to be. For over two years I spent almost 24 hours a day at her bedside, able to go outside for just a few minutes each day. During the day, workmen plied their jackhammers just outside the front door while renovating the complex, while at night I rarely got any good sleep since I needed to lift my mother onto the portable toilet two or three times a night. That combination of factors, along with several others, pushed me to a near-breaking point. I tried meditating and praying, but those felt like band-aid cures compared to the magnitude of the stress I experienced during the remaining hours. The loneliness was crushing, and my body wasn't holding up well either. I've spoken to people who did the caretaking routine not just for two and a half years, as I did, but for ten, fifteen, or even twenty years—and I have no idea how those individuals survived with their sanity intact, if indeed they did. I'm still not sure whether I did.

There was something oddly synchronistic about it all, though, because I realized I was doing for my mother what she had herself done for one of her relatives decades earlier, and in eerily similar ways, too. Like me, she had been housebound for two and half years caretaking her beloved Norwegian aunt Halla (see my painting in chapter three), sounding at times during long-distance-phone calls like she was on the brink of a nervous breakdown—and here I was now doing the same for her, for the exact same length of time, at the same age as she had been at the time, also on the verge of a nervous breakdown. Curious, how family patterns reverberate down through the generations like that sometimes.

The experience pulled me down out of my head and into my emotions in a way I wasn't expecting, nor really prepared for. I felt like I was experiencing a "descent into the underworld" of my own now, except this one wasn't 100 feet down a shaft on the Giza Plateau, or a mile into the Grand Canyon. For years I'd been immersed in the rarified mental atmosphere of symbolism, synchronicity, Egyptian mysteries, astrology, aesthetics, yogic philosophy, and so on—but all that suddenly had to be set aside for hard reality. There wasn't much time for pondering abstract truths or philosophical ruminations, and I couldn't help but wonder if this wasn't some kind of "course correction" provided by fate to help balance things out in my own psyche. Maybe, maybe not.

But as close as I came to a complete breakdown, that never quite happened, and there are a couple of reasons for that. One was that, as tough as it was, I knew that caretaking her was the right thing to do. I could have shuffled her off to a nursing home, but that wasn't a consideration for me. After what she had sacrificed for Halla—not to mention what she'd done for me throughout my life—she didn't deserve that. I can't recall who said it, but someone remarked how you sometimes have to put yourself into unbalance for the sake of love and for the sake of a *greater* balance. I think that's true. More to the point, you can bear up under an awful lot of weight if you believe what you're doing is the right thing.

But there was another reason I made it through that period, and that was music. As claustrophobic and difficult as that period was, music became a healing outlet both my mother and I could turn to for letting off steam. Although she was completely blind, she could still play the piano, and the results were sometimes beautiful works improvised off the top of her head. At times, it sounded like she was channeling harmonies from beyond, since the music was unlike anything she'd composed before. Unbeknownst to her, I recorded some of those improvisations with my camera and posted them on the internet for others to see. When she learned what I had done and the positive responses the videos elicited, she was thrilled to know that people even in faraway places were now able to hear her music.

But she could only sit at the piano for short periods at a time, so I wound up improvising on the piano for *her,* sometimes for hours on end, while she listened from her nearby bed. Things had come full circle, in a way; my early life began with her playing piano for me, while she was pregnant with me, and now here I was at the end of her life, playing piano for her.

Besides just providing entertainment for her, it allowed me to get back in touch with my own creativity. I had played music since I was a child, and hadn't composed anything in years, but two compositions in particular came through me during this time, issuing from complete opposite ends of the musical spectrum. One was a Debussy-inspired piece for harp I called "Open Water," and the other was a more blues-inspired, song called "On My Way Back Now". It almost seemed like both works had been squeezed out of me like toothpaste from a tube, by the pressures of circumstance.

As time went on, my mother became increasingly sweet and childlike, retaining her lucidity but becoming very vulnerable, too. Towards the very end, it seemed as though a veil of sorts had started thinning for her. One day near the start of 2009, she sat up in bed and declared, out of the blue, "There's going to be a big earthquake tomorrow...*I can feel it.*" I didn't give it much thought, but the very next day a major earthquake struck the island of Haiti, not very far south of Florida, killing over 100,000 people.

As it turned out, that wasn't the only earth-shaking event to come. Just one day later, while we were sitting and watching TV together, my mother gasped loudly several times and clutched her chest—and then was gone. It took me completely by surprise, because as elderly as she was, her mind was so clear I felt sure she had several more years ahead of her. In a state of near-panic, I scrambled around trying to find my phone to call someone for help—the hospital, a neighbor, anyone—but I could tell from the color draining out of her face she wasn't coming back. As she lay there, I stroked her hair and whispered how much I loved her, and thanked her for all she had done for me. While waiting for the medical personnel to arrive, I walked over to the nearby piano and played softly for a minute or two, hoping that might somehow ease her transition. My life with her had begun with music, and now it was now ending that way as well, like a circle coming to completion. My brother flew in from Arizona, and after the funeral service we walked out onto the beach after the sun set and scattered both of our parents' ashes out onto the ocean, together.

After he went back to Arizona, I spent the next few days walking along the beach by myself, trying to process all that happened, hoping to gain some perspective on what my life had come to. My serious lack of sleep those previous few years, coupled with the stress and depression I'd been under, left me feeling so drained I couldn't think clearly, not in ordinary ways. But as sometimes happens, breakdowns like that make it possible for important insights to bleed through that thinning veil into consciousness. I was open to *non*-ordinary things now, to bigger concerns and feelings. So while walking along the shoreline one afternoon, I found myself coming back to a question I'd grappled with years before—*Who am I?*

With that, a startling perception emerged. I sensed that this personality of mine, seemingly walking along the beach and feeling sad, was like a marionette puppet, and above it was a much bigger "I" pulling the strings, observing all that was happening as perceived both through my eyes but also from a higher vantage point. This everyday personality and its concerns now seemed very small and fleeting compared to that much bigger "I." Yet there was no sense of judgment or criticality involved in any of this; in fact, it only made me feel more compassionate towards this small, flawed personality, not unlike how one might even feel towards a beloved pet. While that perception itself lasted for just a moment, it was clear, and caused me to me to stop and stand there in silence for several minutes.

I turned to look out at the waves, since they've always held important secrets for me. I waded out until the water reached my waist and stood there for a few moments simply feeling the textures and the coolness flowing around me. The water was cleansing, and the sadness I'd been feeling until then was replaced by a subtle elation. Several moments later, with the currents swirling around me, another question came to mind: *What is a wave?*

Remarkable things, really—waves. They're not the water itself but *a pattern moving through it,* shaping the water as it goes along, similar to how a piece of music shapes and modulates the instruments of an orchestra while being distinct from them. That's true for me, too, I knew; I'm not the atoms or the molecules in this body but a pattern moving through it, exchanging molecules and atoms along the way. In a sense, I *am* music.

And just like that, I move on, as my mother and father continue to move on, and everyone else moves on, rolling like waves across the ocean.

The End

ENDNOTES

(All URLs were accessed in 2020.)

Chapter 2
1. https://www.nytimes.com/2003/03/12/arts/stan-brakhage-avant-garde-filmmaker-is-dead-at-70.html
2. Though I shot thousands of feet of footage during my years at the Art Institute, that ultimately boiled down to just one film, which I began during freshman year but finished after graduating, titled "Awakening." The film was damaged in a flood years later, but I was able to salvage and twice restore roughly half of the film, now re-titled "Awakening III", which I posted at Youtube at https://www.youtube.com/watch?v=C94iiPDcgJk . (Note that the film is silent for the first 45 seconds, after which the musical soundtrack fades in.)

Chapter 6
1. "Myth in the Modern World: An Interview with Wendy Doniger," by Ray Grasse. *The Quest: A Quarterly Journal of Philosophy, Science, Religion, and the Arts*, Winter 1990.

Chapter 12
1. Gordon White, *STAR.SHIPS: A Prehistory of the Spirits*, Scarlett Imprint, 2016, p. 174.
2. Boris claimed that Zahi Hawass was often unscrupulous in his dealings with him through the years, but he managed to find ways of sticking it to the Egyptian in return, sometimes in deviously ingenious ways. Like the time he instigated an elaborate ruse on Zahi with the help of a friend who was a dead-ringer for actress Elizabeth Taylor. Boris knew all-too-well of Zahi's penchant for celebrities—especially beautiful ones—and Boris

decided to exploit that weakness to the hilt. Boris knew in advance that his Liz Taylor lookalike friend would be traveling to Cairo in a few months, and decided to enlist her in a scheme to pull the wool over Zahi's eyes. Boris got his hands on a publicity photograph of Elizabeth Taylor, and upon his friend's arrival convinced her to dress up in a beautiful outfit and make herself up to look as much like the actress as possible. Boris then spread word through an intermediary that the famed actress was in town visiting the ancient monuments, and had her position herself conspicuously at one of the monuments on the plateau where Zahi would certainly learn of her presence. Zahi immediately made his way over to the faux Ms. Taylor, lavishing attention and offering to show her around town. She graciously accepted, of course, and spent the day getting five-star treatment at the finest restaurants and official sites in the city, all under Zahi's fawning tutelage. At day's end, he asked for her autograph; pulling the photo Boris had given her from her purse, she signed it: "to Zahi—from Elizabeth Taylor." "And to this day that photo hangs in Zahi's office," Boris said, roaring with laughter.

3. Robert Temple, *Egyptian Dawn: Exposing the Real Truth Behind Ancient Egypt*, Arrow Books, 2011, pgs. 43-80.
4. Ibid, p. 79.
5. https://web.archive.org/web/20090813082309/http://heritage-key.com/egypt/exclusive-interview-dr-zahi-hawass-indianapolis
6. In early January of 2015, archaeologists announced the discovery of another purported "Tomb of Osiris," this one supposedly built during the 25th Dynasty between 760 and 525 BCE, and located on the west bank of the River Nile near Luxor, Egypt. The fact that there may be more than one Tomb of Osiris should come as no surprise, since any one of them is only a symbolic replica of the original site described in mythology

(although some would argue that the Giza site takes on special significance due to its location on the Plateau). To use a simple analogy, every Christian church that sports an empty crucifix near its altar commemorates the crucifixion and resurrection of Jesus, without claiming to be the actual location of the original event.

ABOUT THE AUTHOR

Ray Grasse is a writer, photographer, and astrologer living in the American Midwest. He is author of several books including *Under a Sacred Sky, An Infinity of Gods, Urban Mystic,* and *Signs of the Times,* and has contributed to many anthologies. His first book, *The Waking Dream,* was called "a masterpiece" by Colin Wilson. He worked on the editorial staffs of Quest Books and The Quest Magazine for 10 years, and has been associate editor of The Mountain Astrologer magazine for over 20 years. He received a degree in filmmaking from the Art Institute of Chicago under Stan Brakhage, and studied under teachers in both the Kriya Yoga and Zen traditions. His websites are www.raygrasse.com and www.raygrassephotography.com

Made in the USA
Monee, IL
08 February 2021

58503235R20118